THE RULES
OF ENGAGEMENT

UNDERSTANDING THE PRINCIPLES
THAT GOVERN THE SPIRITUAL BATTLES IN
OUR LIVES

THE RULES
OF ENGAGEMENT

UNDERSTANDING THE PRINCIPLES
THAT GOVERN THE SPIRITUAL BATTLES IN
OUR LIVES

CHARLES H. KRAFT
AND
DAVID M. DEBORD

WAGNER
PUBLICATIONS

The Rules of Engagement
Copyright © 2000
by Charles H. Kraft and David M. DeBord
ISBN 1-58502-012-5

Published by
Wagner Publications
11005 N. Highway 83
Colorado Springs, CO 80921
www.wagnerpublications.org

Cover design by
Hala Saad
Vision Communications
711 Lowell Street
Dallas, Texas 75214
(214) 827-0620

Edit and Interior design by
Rebecca Sytsema

Rights for publishing this book in other languages are contracted by Gospel Literature International (GLINT). GLINT also provides technical help for the adaptation, translation, and publishing of Bible study resources and books in scores of languages worldwide. For further information, contact GLINT, P.O. Box 4060, Ontario, CA 91761-1003, USA. You may also send e-mail to glintint@aol.com, or visit their web site at www.glint.org.

1 2 3 4 5 6 7 8 9   06 05 04 03 02 01 00

TABLE OF CONTENTS

CHAPTER ONE

TWO KINGDOMS IN CONFLICT

The Battle Scene

"Tal [a captain of the Hosts of Heaven] and his troops gathered again in the little church, and the mood was better this time. They had tasted the first promises of battle; a victory, even though a small one, had been won the night before. Most of all, there were more of them. The original twenty-three had grown to forty-seven as more mighty warriors had gathered, called in by the prayers of ...

"The Remnant!" said Tal with a note of anticipation as he looked over a preliminary list [of church members present] presented to him. ...

Tal read the names. "John and Patricia Coleman—"

Scion [a red-haired, freckled fighter from the British Isles] explained, "They were here last night and spoke up for the preacher. Now they're all the more for him, and they drop to their knees easy as droppin' a hat. We've got them workin'."

"And plenty more, I see," said Tal with a smile. He handed the list to Guilo. "Assign some of our newcomers [angels] to this list. Gather these people in. I want them praying."

Guilo took the list and conferred with several new warriors.

"And what about relatives, friends elsewhere?" Tal asked Scion.

"Plenty o' them are redeemed and ready for prayer. Shall I send emissaries to burden them?"

Tal shook his head. "I can't let any warriors be gone for long. Instead, have messengers carry word to the watchcarers over these people's towns and cities, and let the watchcarers see that these people are burdened with prayer for their loved ones here."

"Done."

Scion set right to work, assigning messengers who immediately vanished to their missions.

Guilo had sent his warriors also and was excited to see the campaign in motion. "I like the feel of this, captain."

"It is a good beginning," Tal said.

"And what of Rafar [one of Satan's lead warriors, also called The Prince of Babylon]? Do you suppose he knows of your presence here?"

"The two of us know each other all too well."

"Then he will be expecting a fight, and soon."

"Which is why we won't fight, not yet. Not until the prayer cover is sufficient and we know why Rafar is here. He's not a prince of small towns but of empires, and he would never be here for any task below his pride. What we've seen is far less than the enemy has planned.

———————◆———————

The outer sentinels saw him approaching and gave an eerie, siren-like wail. Immediately the defenders radiated outward from Rafar's flight path, opening a channel through the defense layers. Rafar swooped skillfully through the channel as demons on all sides saluted him with upheld swords, their glowing eyes like thousands of paired yellow stars on black velvet. He ignored them and passed quickly through. The channel closed again behind him like a living gate.

He floated slowly down through the roof of the house, through the attic, past rafters, walls, plaster, through an upstairs bedroom, through a thick, beam-supported floor and down into a spacious living room below.

The evil in the room was thick and confining, the darkness like black liquid that swirled about with any motion of the limbs. The room was crowded.

"Ba-al Rafar, the Prince of Babylon!" a demon announced from somewhere, and monstrous demons all around the perimeter of the room bowed in respect.

Rafar folded his wings in regal, cape-like fashion and stood with an intimidating air of royalty and might, his jewels flashing impressively. His big yellow eyes studied carefully the orderly ranks of demons lined up all around him. A horrible gathering. These were spirits from the principality levels, princes themselves of their own nations, peoples, tribes. Some were from Africa, some were from the Orient, several were from Europe. All were invincible. Rafar noted their tremendous size and formidable appearance; they all matched him for size and ferocity, and he doubted he would ever venture to challenge any of them. To receive a bow from them was a great honor, a compliment indeed.

"Hail, Rafar," said a gargling voice from the end of the room.

The Strongman. It was forbidden to speak his name. He was one of the few majesties intimate with Lucifer himself—a vicious global tyrant responsible over the centuries for resisting the plans of the living God and establishing Lucifer's kingdom on the earth. Rafar and his kind controlled nations; those such as the Strongman controlled Rafar and his kind.

———————◆———————

Rafar could hear the praise from where he stood on the hill above the town, and he glowered at these saints of God. Let them whine over their fallen pastor. Their singing would be curtailed soon enough when the Strongman and his hordes arrived.

Countless spirits were arriving in the town of Ashton— but they were not the kind Rafar desired. They rushed in under the ground, they filtered in under the cover of occasional clouds, they sneaked in by riding invisibly in cars, trucks, vans, buses. In hiding places all over the town one warrior would be joined by another, those two would be joined by two more, those four would be joined by four. They too could hear the singing. They could feel the strength coursing through them with every note. Their swords droned with the resonance of the worship. It was the worship and the prayers of these saints that had called them here in the first place. (Excerpts taken from *This Present Darkness*).[1]

The Backdrop of the Battle

Even before time began, a cosmic drama, not unlike the fictional one depicted above, had already played itself out in the heavenlies, establishing the spiritual forces that would vie for human allegiance. The biblical record of Isaiah 14 paints the heavenly picture. Lucifer, the archangel, had stood at the right hand of God, exercising the full authority of the Father in the affairs of the Creation. No higher position existed. Lucifer's power and authority were only exceeded by that of the Creator Himself. But Isaiah's story accounts a violent rending of the relationship between Lucifer and the Father. Isaiah says Lucifer's desire was "to climb up to heaven and to place his throne above the highest stars . . . where he would sit like a king . . . he would be like God" (14:13-14). What Isaiah doesn't tell us is what triggered this reaction in Lucifer. Whatever it was, the result was Lucifer's expulsion from heaven along with a significant number of angels, who chose to follow his lead. Something had obviously gone wrong in Paradise.

God's Plan: Human Dominion

A clue to the cause of Lucifer's rebellion may be found in Psalm 8:5, where the Psalmist records that God created humans "a little lower than God himself." While historically most translators record here that humans were created "a little lower than the angels," this seems to be a translation rooted more in a preconceived and historical theological mindset than linguistics. The more accurate translation suggests that in creation order, humans were placed above the angels, including Satan.

It is, therefore, plausible to consider that the root of Lucifer's rebellion was that his honored place closest to God was, by God's own design, usurped by the new beings—hence the jealous and destructive rebellion that followed. This displacement would also explain Lucifer's avowed hatred of people. The stated purpose of Satan's rule then became the destruction of God's Creation, and especially the destruction of human beings as the central object of God's love in Creation.

By God's plan, humankind was to have dominion over all the created order (Gen. 1:28). But men and women were also created to be in intimate relationship with the Father, to "walk with Him in the cool of the evening." God had placed only one requirement on humans in return for their place of dominion over the earth—they must obey the rules God set in place. The one rule mentioned in Genesis 2 was that Adam and Eve not eat of the Tree of the Knowledge of Good and Evil planted in the Garden. The punishment for disobedience was death (Gen. 2:17), not literal death, but "relational death" due to a separation from the Father and loss of dominion over Creation.

Unfortunately, Adam and Eve didn't grasp the seriousness of their decision to disobey. Like all sin, it was a loss that had to be experienced before the larger result would be known—a result Satan knew, but wisely hid as he orchestrated the temptation. Hence, Satan's strategy in the Garden became the subversion of God's plan—to seize for himself what God had given to humankind as a gift.

Satan's Plan: Dominion by Deceit

The Tempter came in skillfully, looking for the weakness in humankind's defense. Not willing to reveal his stake in the deal, he focused on an attractive deception that would lead the first humans to believe they were unjustly being denied something great. The enemy still presents sin in this way. Doubt was his weapon of choice this time: he simply questioned God's motives in requiring specific obedience. "You will not surely die," he said, and the seed of doubt was sown. Then he dangled the carrot, "You will be like God and know what is good and what is bad." "You will be like God ... (Gen. 3:4)." Why would those who have everything want more? Isn't it curious the way temptation always seems to appear at the exact point of our weakness?

"Created a little lower than God ..." Yet Adam squandered our position in Creation. Temptation came. Adam disobeyed. God exposed his sin. Punishment had to be swift. "Death" came in the form of expulsion from the Garden where our ancestors had complete dominion. In Adam's disobedience, we went from owning everything to owning nothing, from a life of no effort, to a life of sweat, toil, and pain. Because of sin, from now on, men would have to sweat for their daily bread and women would suffer in childbirth and have strife with men.

Then the real tragedy of his sin emerged; the part Darkness had kept secret. Not only did humans fall from their place of dominion, all Creation fell with them. That which was hidden was then revealed, to the horror of all. Into our vacated position of dominion came the Tempter, Lucifer, now named Satan.

What had been created "good"—God's Creation—now became cursed and dominated by Satan. What had not been revealed previously was the high stakes that were on the table. Now Satan would be legitimately able to say to Jesus later, "It has all been handed over to me" (Luke 4:6). God trusted Adam. But Adam failed the character test, and God lost His Creation to Satan. The one who had wanted a throne for himself, now had it. The Earth was his and all that dwelt therein ... at least for a season.

Satan's Kingdom: The Rule of Evil

Having claimed the spoils of his victory, Satan set himself up as the lord of this earthly kingdom. Scripture calls him by various titles: "the evil god of this world" (II Cor. 4:4), "the ruler of this world" (John 14:30), "the rule of the Evil One" (I John 5:19). While he had gained his position by deceit, he ruled as if by divine right. But it must be noted that while Satan ascended his new throne and claimed his new title, he was powerless in and of himself. The power Satan exercised had originated from God the Father; therefore, Satan ruled earth with delegated authority.

Originally Satan's power and authority came from God in his position as Archangel. For reasons only God knows He allowed Satan to retain his power when he rebelled and was thrown out of heaven. But there was another distressing piece of information the Deceiver knew, yet did not reveal until forced to do so—one day the Messiah, the Chosen One of God, would come to reclaim the Creation and restore it and humankind to the Father (Gen. 3:15).

Jesus would come one day and reestablish humanity to its rightful place of dominion over the earth. Satan didn't know when this time would be, but it was an inevitability for which he must prepare. If Adam could be deceived, perhaps the Messiah could also. In the meantime, there was work to be done. If he couldn't keep his position as lord of the earth, he would then destroy as much of it as he could, along with those that inhabited it.

To accomplish his task, Satan organized his kingdom of "dark angels" into a hierarchy of authority. Since he is not omnipresent like God, he needed a chain of command to carry out his strategies. Ephesians 6:12 suggests several layers of evil forces serving under Satan's command, doing his bidding. Some believe that Revelation 12:4 indicates that one third of God's angels followed Satan out of heaven. Only God knows what that number literally is, how much power Satan actually has and what its limits are. Based on the damage done in the name of evil, the amount of power and the number of demons serving him must be substantial.

God's Kingdom: The Rule of Love

"In the fullness of time, Jesus came," reports the Apostle Luke in his Gospel account of the birth of Jesus (Luke 2:6). This powerful statement ushers in God's intent to redeem His Creation from the clutches of the Evil One. It boldly declares that even while God was allowing Satan to set up his power base in the created order, He had a plan already in place to retake it from the enemy.

This declaration, "in the fullness of time," declares that when the divine time was right, when the Father had everything in place that needed to be in place, He would launch His counteroffensive on earth and in the heavenlies. He did this in the person of Jesus Christ, His Son, the Messiah, who came to earth to demonstrate the Father's love to a disenfranchised humankind.

In the coming of Jesus to earth, the kingdom of God was ushered into human history. The kingdom of God meant the reign and rule of God in the hearts of humankind was now present. It was to be our weapon in the war to retake Creation. Insights into the kingdom of God, what it looked and acted like, filled the teachings of Jesus. He demonstrated it, illustrated it and commanded his disciples to live it in their lives. At His resurrection, He released the kingdom of God to His disciples, commanding them to spread it around the world.

The Kingdom and its participants were empowered by the Holy Spirit the same way that Jesus was empowered by the Holy Spirit at His baptism. With Kingdom power in hand, embodied in the Holy Spirit, Jesus' disciples were empowered to take on the enemy first hand and do the things that Jesus did to defeat him. Jesus' prediction to His own disciples was directive and inclusive: "Everything you saw me do you will do and more" (John 14:12).

Two Kingdoms in Conflict: The Ongoing Scene of Battle

Having identified the two sides in the battle, the war now rages—over us in the heavenlies, around us in the natural world, and inside us in our bodies, souls, and spirits—all simultaneously. On one side the forces of evil stand poised, intent on retaining the rule of this world and the reign of darkness. On the other side stand those with allegiance to the kingdom of God and its Savior.

While Satan relies on his army of fallen angels to deceive people into accomplishing his destructive purposes, God chooses to indwell and trust human beings, the very ones who created this problem in the first place. Surprisingly, for reasons only He knows, it is a valued part of God's strategy for humans to play a vital role in reestablishing His Kingdom in Creation. With Jesus as our model, we have seen demonstrated the power available to us. Just as Jesus, the Second Adam, warred with Satan while on earth, so we also are to war with Satan. And our power is the same power that Jesus relied on—the power coming from the filling of the Holy Spirit.

This was the powerful Kingdom secret that Jesus demonstrated but that most believers have never known. The Kingdom power demonstrated by Jesus was not found in His Divinity, but in obedience—that same obedience abandoned in the Garden, resulting in sin. In obedience, Jesus put His Divinity aside when He came in human flesh. That is why He did no public miracles until after His baptism by John the Baptist. During that public consecration, done in obedience to the Father's will, the Holy Spirit came upon Him. Only then did Jesus enter the battle to retake Creation.

What Jesus did He had to do without Divinity. Otherwise, how could His followers be expected to do the same things He did? They certainly had no Divinity in themselves. Therefore, Jesus had to call them, teach them, and train them. And just as He had not ministered until power came on Him, He told them at His Ascension not to do anything until the gift of the Holy Spirit had been imparted to them also. Only after that happened (Acts 1:8), did the battle begin in earnest.

The battle between the kingdom of God and the kingdom of Satan still rages. Though defeated at the Cross, Satan and his army of fallen angels refuse to admit defeat and are fighting to retain control of the Creation through seeking and holding onto the hearts and minds of humankind.

But the soldiers of the kingdom of God march under the mandate of the Savior: "to bring good news to the poor ... proclaim liberty to the captives ... recovery of sight to the blind ... to free the oppressed ... and announce that the time has come when the Lord will save his people" (Luke 4:18-19). The satanic manifesto driving the fallen angels counters it: "steal, kill, and destroy" (John 10:10).

Our Battle Strategy:
Offensive and Defensive

As soldiers of the kingdom of God our battle strategy is both defensive and offensive. It is defensive in that we are to be prepared for war, not a war such as the world fights, but a spiritual war; not against flesh and blood, but against wicked demonic beings in space (Eph. 2:2, 6:12). We are called "to put on the whole armor of God" (Eph. 6:10-20). We are to protect ourselves, using all the authority that the Father has given us. But the battle is also offensive; we are to be looking for "captives" to set free. Captives are those who are trapped in Satan's deception, trapped by their allegiance to the darkness. Whether they are in darkness by their own choices or for lack of Light, Jesus calls us to set them free, to bring Light to the Darkness. Sometimes we may be the very captives who need freedom!

It is to this battle that we now turn our attention. The portion of the battle that is most crucial to know and understand is the rules that seem to govern it. More specifically, we need to know and understand the rules that govern the spirit beings who fight with us, the angels of the kingdom of God; and the spirit beings warring against us, the dark angels of Satan's army.

It appears that the same rules and principles govern both sides. Therefore, if we are to be victorious, we must begin to discover what the rules of engagement are in the battle that consumes us. The demonic spirits we battle certainly know what the rules are and use them to their advantage against us. And for us, unfortunately, ignorance of the rules or even of the battle that is raging against us does not protect us from its results.

Notes

1. Frank Peretti, *This Present Darkness* (Wheaton, IL: Crossways Books, 1986), pp. 119-120, 132, 325.

◆————

CHAPTER TWO

THE COSMIC DRAMA: GOOD VS. EVIL

Worldview: It's All in How You See It! . . . Or Is It?

The Bible assumes that the spirit world, the human world, and the material world are all interconnected. This is the worldview of both the Old and New Testaments. The people in Biblical times assumed an interaction between spirit beings (their gods) and their world, which included their possessions, crops, and fertility.

This is easily seen in the proliferation of pagan gods and worship centers focused on territorial rights, fertility, protection, healing, and the like in biblical societies. For agrarian societies, crop failure or other misfortune could mean starvation. The writers of the Bible wrote with this perspective as a basic assumption. They didn't question the belief that spirit beings, including demonic entities, populate the spirit world and interact with humans for both good and evil purposes.

The Apostle Paul was so conscious of the continuous interaction between human and spirit worlds, that he saw no need to explain it. He knew his hearers were "not unaware of [Satan's] schemes" (II Cor. 2:11).

For several generations, however, western societies have largely not believed in, or at the very least, ignored the supernatural world. Enlightenment philosophy and scientism came to dominate the centers of learning, affecting both scholars and the common people, secularizing their thinking to the extent that most believed that if something could not be explained rationally and proven scientifically, it did not exist.

The supernatural world, of which western peoples were very conscious, came to be excluded from the contemporary worldview. Even in the church the supernatural worldview of the first century church came largely to be seen as antiquated and "primitive" and, therefore, superceded by modern scientific perspectives. Modern society had just become too sophisticated, too educated, to embrace "primitive superstitions."

Theologically, both dispensationalists and Reformed theologians have contended that signs and wonders were pretty well limited to the first century as a kind of special dispensation from God. They are, therefore, no longer available to us. Such theologians displaced belief in spiritual power and miracles in the minds of most members of mainline and evangelical denominations. With it also disappeared most interest in things related to spiritual warfare. Theology had been conformed to cultural beliefs rather than to biblical truths.

To the "sophisticated" western mind it was easier to focus on the material, human world that could be observed, studied, and described. This approach resulted in explosive growth in both physical and social (human) sciences. Only with the advent of the New Age Movement in the mid-twentieth century did the study of, and interaction with, the spirit world regain some social acceptability and a fresh resurgence of interest. This counterfeit spirituality has been embraced by many for which the church has done no better than secular society at meeting spiritual needs. It is, however, the product of the enemy of God—Satan.

For Easterners the existence of the spirit world and spirit beings had never been in question. Eastern religions birthed much of the New Age spirituality and teachings. But for Westerners there had been a virtual blindness to both the existence and influence of spiritual beings and spiritual power in human experience. Hence the seductive nature of the New Age Movement. Many Westerners, longing for spiritual experiences to quench the God-created spiritual thirst, yet unwilling to embrace the tired, powerless Christianity of most Western churches, quickly embraced the spiritual "knowledge" and "self-realization" of the New Age.

Western intellectual arrogance, fueled by scientific and philosophical "sophistication," mandated that demonic spirit beings be seen merely as the creation of primitive and superstitious minds to explain what they could not explain rationally. However, when New Age thinking came along, "enlightened minds" quickly embraced the practice of seeking "spirit guides" to show them "truths" in the search for spiritual knowledge and spiritual "enlightenment." New Agers were now unknowingly inviting the very entities they would have denied existed (demons) to be their spiritual teachers. Reacting to intellectual arrogance and spiritual ignorance, the demonic kingdom merely renamed demons, calling them "spirit guides" and "sages," and had them channel the "truth of the ages" through seduced, deceived mediums and teachers. Wherever there is a spiritual void, people or something will seek to fill it.

The Spirit World:
A Reality, Not an Option

Reality is that there is a spirit world out there whether we believe in it or not! And there is a God-placed yearning within humankind not only to believe in, but also to connect with, this spirit world. This yearning helps explain the incredible growth in popularity of new television shows such as "Touched By an Angel" or the increased angelic theme of many new Hollywood movies and TV scripts. There is even the emergence of commercial businesses that traffic only in angel merchandise.

People are hungry for a touch of the supernatural. There is a deep spiritual hunger within each of us, put there by God to draw us to Him. Hence the seductive draw of counterfeit spirituality and "enlightened" teachers who promise new "truths and knowledge from the past" and a connection to the spirit world. Moreover, New Age practitioners deliver on their promises, thanks to the work of demons from which they get their "spiritual" powers. Satan is committed to pervert anything that God seeks to do for His Creation. Unfortunately for most of the naive seekers in this camp, the connection made through New Age sources is to the dark side of the spirit world masquerading as light, not to the Light and Truth that it advertises. Only God can give us that.

So what stands before us is a great "Cosmic Drama"—the unfolding of a continuous battle between the forces of Light, representing God and His Kingdom, and the forces of evil, representing Satan and his kingdom. The angels carry out God's plans by fighting for His people and Creation (Heb. 1:14). Meanwhile, the demons serve Satan by fighting against God's people and His purpose.

Discovering the Rules:
The Challenge We Face

A major challenge before us as believers is to discover and identify the rules that govern this cosmic battle. Some of these rules are illustrated in the selection from the novel *This Present Darkness* quoted at the beginning of this book. Our goal for the remainder of the book will be to identify the principles and guidelines we have discovered so far that seem to govern the relationships between the spirit world and the human world.

In identifying these "ground rules" we are suggesting that God, as a part of His Creation, has dictated principles or rules that govern the spirit world as surely as He dictated rules and laws that govern the natural order. Identifying such principles will reduce our ignorance and increase our ability to succeed in the "cosmic battle" that engulfs us. Knowing what the rules of engagement are certainly removes the surprise advantage the enemy has had over us to this point.

In no way do we suggest that this is a definitive list of "ground rules." We are just at the start of our quest to identify the rules. Later publications, we hope, will expand on and improve our list. We intend, though, that this be a step toward developing a "science" in the spirit realm parallel to the sciences already developed to deal with human and material aspects of God's Creation.

The overall assumption, from which the following principles flow, is that *God has built regularities into the ways in which the spiritual and human spheres interact.* Since science is the study of regularities, we conclude that a spiritual "branch" can be built that focuses on these areas. From here, theories can be advanced, tested and modified by those who have gone beyond the elementary levels of thinking about and experiencing spiritual warfare. Pooling our thoughts and experience can increase our knowledge base and subsequent understanding.

We had best become serious students of these rules because the demons we fight against already know the rules, and use them to their advantage. Learning the rules will at least put us on level ground with the demonic realm. And with the authority and power Jesus has already given his believers added to the plan, we will have the winning edge.

The General Principles Ordering the Battle

Charles Kraft developed the first draft of these spiritual warfare principles in *Behind Enemy Lines*.[1] The principles and accompanying observations developed then were a first effort at trying to codify an overview of how the spiritual kingdoms, both God's and Satan's, function and interact. They initially grew out of his study of Scripture and the practice of ministry. Since that time we have tried to be good "scientists" by testing these principles and refining them under "battlefield conditions." This process has led to the revision of some of the original principles and the addition of others. We hope this refining process will continue as others add their observations to ours.

We have identified six general rules or "principles" at work. We will devote a chapter to each principle. Following the description of each principle will be a series of "observations" that illustrate various applications of that principle in spiritual warfare. We have used a numbering system for the observations for easy reference. The principles and observations reflect implications for both individuals and institutions. Following is an overview of the principles and observations we will discuss:

THE GROUND RULES OF SPIRITUAL WARFARE

———————◆———————

PRINCIPLE ONE: There are two dispensers of suprahuman spiritual power—God and Satan

OBSERVATION 1.1—God is the originator of all spiritual laws, principles, and structures.

OBSERVATION 1.2—Satan can only copy, counterfeit, or pervert what God has created for His purposes.

OBSERVATION 1.3—The two dispensers of spiritual power, God and Satan, are not equal in power.

OBSERVATION 1.4—Satan can gain permission from God to go beyond his set limits and boundaries.

OBSERVATION 1.5—Satan can hinder God's workings.

OBSERVATION 1.6—Angels, including Satan, are below humans in the created order.

OBSERVATION 1.7—Satan gained authority over Creation from Adam.

OBSERVATION 1.8—There are spirit beings, arranged hierarchically, that serve either God or Satan.

OBSERVATION 1.9—It is clear from Scripture that spirit beings are very active and influential in the human arena.

———————◆———————

PRINCIPLE TWO: There is a very close relationship between the spiritual and human realms.

OBSERVATION 2.1—Any analysis of a given event in the human sphere needs to take into account both human and spiritual influences.

OBSERVATION 2.2—The principles governing the relationship between the human world and the spirit world seem to be essentially the same for both kingdoms.

OBSERVATION 2.3—The choices made by human beings affect their relationships with God and Satan.

OBSERVATION 2.4—In the human realm, God has limited His ability to protect us against evil.

OBSERVATION 2.5—The effects of a commitment or dedication of a human being to God or Satan are carried down generationally through that person's descendants.

OBSERVATION 2.6—Through our allegiance to God or Satan, spirit beings gain influence for the expression of power and control in the lives of human beings.

OBSERVATION 2.7—The rights given by people to spirit powers extend to people's property and territory.

———◆———

PRINCIPLE THREE: There are major differences between how God and Satan operate.

OBSERVATION 3.1—God works with integrity; Satan works by deception.

OBSERVATION 3.2—God leads His followers to freedom; Satan leads his followers into captivity.

OBSERVATION 3.3—God inhabits His people with His Holy Spirit. The best Satan can do is inhabit his people with some of his angels, called demons.

OBSERVATION 3.4—Satan can use God's laws and biblical principles to accomplish his purposes in the human realm.

OBSERVATION 3.5—Those committed to God adopt the character of God; those committed to Satan adopt the character of Satan.

OBSERVATION 3.6—God can be trusted; Satan cannot.

OBSERVATION 3.7—God offers the genuine; Satan can only counterfeit.

OBSERVATION 3.8—God offers us a "true self" while Satan offers us a "false self."

OBSERVATION 3.9—God can override His rules for Creation; Satan cannot override God's rules.

——————◆——————

PRINCIPLE FOUR: The obtaining and exercising of spiritual power and authority by humans flows from allegiance, relationship, and obedience to either God or Satan.

OBSERVATION 4.1—God and Satan can invest people, places and things with power.

OBSERVATION 4.2—There are certain limitations to what God and Satan can do in the human realm. These limitations are related to the cooperation God and Satan receive from humans.

OBSERVATION 4.3—To accomplish their purposes, God and Satan ordinarily work in the human realm through partnerships with humans.

OBSERVATION 4.4—Through human allegiance and obedience, God and Satan gain legal rights to work in human affairs.

OBSERVATION 4.5—Rituals such as sacrifice, worship, and prayer seem to enable God or Satan.

OBSERVATION 4.6—Through blood sacrifices, power is

released to the followers of God and Satan.

OBSERVATION 4.7—The spirit world works within the human world according to authority relationships.

OBSERVATION 4.8—Humans can be inhabited either by God's Spirit, demons, or both.

OBSERVATION 4.9—Both God and Satan are able to provide protection for their followers.

OBSERVATION 4.10—There is a relationship between the amount of human support God or Satan has and the ability of each to successfully attack the opposing kingdom.

OBSERVATION 4.11—Those related to God or Satan can use a variety of methods to transmit spiritual power.

OBSERVATION 4.12—People have the right to switch from one allegiance to the other.

———————◆———————

PRINCIPLE FIVE: Cultural forms can be empowered.

OBSERVATION 5.1—Physical objects can be dedicated to spirit beings.

OBSERVATION 5.2—Words used with the authority of God or Satan, especially blessings or curses, are empowered to release reward or punishment in the human realm.

OBSERVATION 5.3—Other nonmaterial, cultural forms can also be empowered by God or Satan.

OBSERVATION 5.4—Buildings can be invested with spiritual power by God or Satan.

OBSERVATION 5.5—Animals can be empowered with spiritual power.

—————◆—————

PRINCIPLE 6: Territories and organizations can be subject to spirit power.

OBSERVATION 6.1—God or Satan's cosmic-level spirits seem to exert a "force field" influence over territories, buildings, and organizations.

OBSERVATION 6.2—Spirit beings must have legal rights to exert authority over territories, buildings, organizations and individuals.

OBSERVATION 6.3—The rules for breaking the power of cosmic-level satanic spirits are parallel to those for breaking the power of ground-level satanic spirits over individuals.

OBSERVATION 6.4—Cosmic-level spirits seem to wield their authority over territories as defined by humans.

OBSERVATION 6.5—Cosmic-level spirits seem to be assigned to human organizations, institutions and activities.

OBSERVATION 6.6—There are rules that can be followed to launch attacks upon evil spirits or God's angels assigned to territories and organizations.

Notes

1. Charles Kraft, *Behind Enemy Lines* (Ann Arbor, MI: Servant Publications, 1994), pp. 31-62.

CHAPTER THREE

♦

PRINCIPLE ONE:
There Are Two Dispensers of Suprahuman Spiritual Power— God and Satan

God the Father is the ultimate source of all power and authority. In Satan's original role as Lucifer, the Archangel, God had given him great power to perform his role. When Lucifer led his rebellion against God, in what we believe was his reaction to humankind's creation above him in the created order (Ezek. 28:11-19, Is. 14:12-15), it appears that God allowed him to keep the power He had given him. Why this was allowed, only God knows. Satan then used that delegated power to establish his evil kingdom and organize his demonic troops. This delegated authority then is the source of the evil power emanating from the demonic kingdom.

Observation 1.1
God is the originator of all spiritual laws, principles, and structures.

These spiritual realities are a part of God's creation as are the laws, principles, and structures governing the human and material worlds. Since Satan is sterile, he has no creative powers. To accomplish his purposes, therefore, he takes what God created for good and uses it for evil. Just as God designed a hierarchical type organization among His angels (archangel, messengers, warriors, heralds) so Satan fashioned a hierarchy among his angels (rulers, authorities, powers, principalities, spiritual forces [Eph 6:12]).

Just as God's desire is for the allegiance of the hearts of humankind, so Satan desires that same goal. Just as God requires obedience from those who would have a relationship with Him and be recipients of His authority and protection, so Satan demands obedience from those who are under him and who receive his power and protection. Just as God empowers words for good through blessings, so Satan empowered words for evil through curses.

Observation 1.2
Satan can only copy, counterfeit or pervert what God has created for His purposes.

Even though Satan is a created being, he is sterile and, unlike God, cannot create something from nothing. This appears to be the case with all spirit beings. This may give us additional insight into what fueled Satan's rebellion against God, since only humans were given the ability to "be fruitful and multiply." While Satan cannot create anything, he is creative in the development of his strategies against us. All living things have an innate, creative ability to adjust and change when needed, and Satan is no different.

Satan, by masquerading as one of God's angels (II Cor. 11:14), is able to counterfeit much of what only God can give. He will offer people such things as happiness, comfort, success, money, power, or whatever else they might want. The promise of free drugs and illicit sex initially draws many people into satanic cults. He offers these things because they are parallel to many of the things that God created as good gifts for His people—such as intimacy and joy. The difference in Satan's gifts, however, is that the gift offered is always temporary, with the aim of ensnaring, deceiving, and enslaving the person receiving the gift.

Satan's kingdom is a counterfeit. It is buttressed by deceit in place of truth, the delegated power of a rebellious archangel in place of the power that comes from God Himself. It is full of promises that he cannot keep, blessings that turn into curses, darkness in place of light, death in place of life. Satan even has enough delegated power to perform certain signs and wonders (remember Pharaoh's magicians), though the Apostle Paul calls them lying signs and wonders (II Thes. 2:9-10).

Observation 1.3
The two dispensers of spiritual power, God and Satan, are not equal in power.

Although both kingdoms have power, their power is not equal. While other religions allow for multiple gods of equal power, the Judeo-Christian belief allows for only one God, Jehovah, who is all-powerful. In his rebellion, Lucifer took an unknown number of angels with him, angels who believed his lie that he would rise above God. We assume, however, that God's warriors considerably outnumber those of the enemy.

Because Satan has power only as long as God allows him to have it, and to the extent that He allows, that power is confined within the rules the Father has built into the creation. And, since Jesus' resurrection, Satan's true position is one of defeat. Scripture indicates that Jesus "made a public spectacle" of Satan and led him "as a captive in [Jesus'] victory procession" (Col. 2:15). Satan had claimed his victory over the Father in the destruction of Jesus on the Cross. But the resurrection made his victory short-lived. Today he only wins battles; the outcome of the war has already been decided. The Cross and Empty Tomb are the victory symbols.

Observation 1.4
Satan can gain permission from God to go beyond his set limits and boundaries.

The story of Job illustrates this observation. It shows the fact that God has put restrictions on what Satan can do in the natural and material worlds. But it also reveals that God can grant permission for Satan to do his evil work outside of the established limits (Job 1:9-12). Why God would allow this is not explained. All of us have seen people who seem to be on the receiving end of more than their share of Satan's attacks. It's as if Satan continually keeps them in his sights, and life for them is a continuous struggle filled with pain and turmoil.

Scripture does not explain this, but addresses instead the questionings of Job. God says, "Job, were you there when I created the world? Did you contribute one thing to creation" (Job 38:1-40:1)? The implication is "Job, this is all bigger than you. If I am able to create whatever I desire, why can't you trust Me with what is happening to you? Can you accept that I know what is happening to you and that My plan for you is bigger than your immediate circumstance?" Job's response was the appropriate one: "I am unworthy—how can I reply to You?"

This observation also considers the oft-asked question of any prayer minister: "Where was Jesus when this bad thing was happening to me? Why did God let this happen to me?" We will address this recurring question more fully in Observation 2.4.

Observation 1.5
Satan can hinder God's workings.

In Daniel 10, we have the amazing story of just such a thing happening. In response to Daniel's prayer, an angel was dispatched immediately to deliver God's answer. But God's angel was "blocked" for three weeks by one of Satan's angels, a high-level spirit named the "Prince of Persia." After a three-week standoff, it took the intervention of Michael, God's Archangel, to help the messenger angel fight his way through to Daniel (Dan. 10:12-13).

We are left to ponder how often the answers to our prayers are held up in much the same way, as Satan assigns his angels to interfere with God's angels bringing God's answer to our prayers! If God always got His way, as some popular theologies would contend, everyone would be saved (2 Peter 3:9) and Jesus would not have instructed us to pray "may your Kingdom come; may your will be done on earth as it is in heaven" (Matt. 6:10). His will would simply be accomplished because He wanted it.

Observation 1.6
Angels, including Satan, are below humans in the created order.

This statement is supported by the fact that we are the only created beings bearing God's image (Gen. 1:26). The correct translation of Psalm 8:5 states that we were created inferior only to God (Elohim) Himself. The *Good News Bible* reads, "You made [humans] inferior only to yourself (Elohim)." No angel/spirit being is created in God's image. No angel/spirit being can create living souls in God's image. Only humanity is compatible for God to unite with as He did in the incarnation of Jesus.

When Adam fell, however, he obeyed Satan, thus giving Satan rights over both humans and the world God had given to Adam. (These are the rights Satan claimed in Luke 4:6.) Because of his sin, Adam lost his favored position in Creation and descended to a lower rank than Satan and his angels. Consequently, we read in Hebrews 2:7 that Jesus came to live "for a little while lower than the angels." From this position Jesus, as the Second Adam (I Cor. 15:45-47), won back humankind's rightful place in Creation, a place above the angels. Thus, we battle against the angels of darkness from a superior position. Satan and his demons know this. It is probably why he works so hard to make us think otherwise.

Observation 1.7
Satan gained authority over Creation from Adam.

In the fall, Adam forfeited his place of dominion as lord over the earth and all living things to Satan. Satan knew this inversion was the real prize as he began to tempt Eve. Therefore, in the Temptation of Jesus, Satan was legitimately offering Jesus dominion over the earth, because it was his to give (Luke 4:6). This point further indicates why the author of Hebrews says that Jesus came to live "for a little while lower than the angels" (Heb. 2:7). Having set aside His Divinity, Jesus chose to live as we do in a world taken over by Satan and his angels.

So as the Second Adam, who shed His blood on the Cross, Jesus bought back the created order and restored it to its original position. Through His faithfulness, He restored our position of lordship over the created order, though we have not yet seen that victory consummated in the final locking up of the usurper, Satan.

Observation 1.8
There are spirit beings, arranged hierarchically, that serve either God or Satan.

Both sides of the spirit world seem to be ordered hierarchically, with each level being assigned an appropriate degree of power and authority. Again, power is delegated, passed down from God. Some angels have names that relate to their rank, (e.g. the "archangels" Michael and Gabriel), while others draw their name from their function (e.g. spirit of fear, spirit of witchcraft). On God's side we hear of cherubim and seraphim in addition to archangels and angels. On Satan's side we find titles such as princes, principalities, rulers, authorities, cosmic powers, and demons.

Angels, whether God's or Satan's, take orders from their master. They are not creative beings like God or humans and so do not reproduce or have the ability to create something from nothing (Matt. 22:30). And though they both know the past, their knowledge of the future and of God's plans is limited. Perhaps this is why angels and demons have such an interest in the affairs of humans (Matt. 24:36, Luke 15:10, I Tim. 5:21). The only thing about the future that demons know for sure is that their side has lost the war; all demons know about the Cross and the meaning of the Empty Tomb.

Observation 1.9
It is clear from Scripture that spiritual beings are very active and influential in the human arena.

The primary rule operating here is that good and evil angels act only on behalf of their master. But to act, angels need either Satan or God's permission or a conscious or unconscious invitation from human beings. For example, in order for demons to live within a person they need a legal right granted by that person, someone in authority over that person or a generational entry point.

Satan's angels are commissioned to diminish or destroy God's reign in the lives of people. They prefer, however, to keep people from discovering the kingdom of God in the first place. To accomplish this they tempt, disrupt, harass, destroy, and kill (John 10:10). God's angels, on the other hand, are assigned to protect (Matt. 18:10), perhaps to govern (Rev. 1-3), to bear God's messages to His people (Gen. 22:11-12; Num. 22:31-35; Dan. 10:13), and to fight Satan's angels (Dan. 10:12-13). We have recently participated in a ministry session where a person actually saw an angel who was the agent of God's healing in her life.

One can only ponder the effect demons have had on human history by their ability to influence and turn people's thoughts toward evil. The Holocaust is but one example of the power of this demonic influence, a power that was unleashed in one man, and through him infected a nation. This infection resulted in the slaughter of millions of precious men, women and children. Considering the hatred the enemy has towards God, it is no wonder that over six million of these dead were God's chosen people, the Jews.

CHAPTER FOUR

———— ◆ ————

PRINCIPLE TWO:
There Is a Very Close Relationship Between the Spiritual and the Human Realms

What humans do on earth seems to affect what happens in the spirit world ... and vice-versa. Examples abound in Scripture reflecting this truth. Adam's first sin impacted his relationships within both the spiritual and earthly realm (Satan took Adam's place as lord of the earth, Adam lost his intimate relationship with God and Adam lost his position over Creation). When Cain killed his brother, Abel's blood "[cried] out to [God] from the ground, like a voice calling for revenge" (Gen. 4:10). A good example of this close relationship at the individual level is when King Saul gave in to human jealousy and became demonized (I Kings 18:6-10). Dark angels always stand ready and willing to take advantage of any opportunity to invade those who give them legal rights to do so.

This principle is also applicable on a national level. When taking the Promised Land, Israel fought her enemies on land while Yahweh fought the gods (cosmic-level demons) of

Israel's enemies in the heavenlies. Israel won battles whenever they obeyed Yahweh, but lost battles whenever they disobeyed Him. This is seen graphically in the battle between the Israelites and Moabites recorded in II Kings 3. Israel was defeating the Moabite army in spectacular fashion, having driven their enemy army back into its walled city. After the king of Moab attempted unsuccessfully to escape with seven hundred of his soldiers, he took his firstborn son and, in an act of desperation, sacrificed him on the wall of the city as an offering to the god of Moab (II Kings 3:27).

This act of sacrificial, ritual killing released so much demonic power that the Moabites, who were losing the battle, suddenly turned back the Israelites. The Israelites, stunned by what had happened, and realizing the power of it, "returned to their own country" without consulting God. They regrettably didn't even try to claim the spiritual power God would have been willing to unleash to overcome the demonic power released by the sacrifice of the king's oldest child and heir.

Bringing this national application closer to home, one can only wonder at the demonic power that has been released over the United States since the legalization of abortion in 1973. How many millions of innocent infants have been sacrificed since this time in the name of convenience? And how often is the act of abortion used in a first-time pregnancy, aborting the very child who would have become a firstborn child and an heir? Add to that the United States Supreme Court's decision to remove prayer from public schools in 1962 and we begin to see an interesting parallel.

Ponder the relationship between these examples, the simultaneous decline in morality and family values and the rise in humanistic and New Age trends that have taken place in the United States since the early '60s. Indeed, the sacrifice of innocents has once again been used to empower darkness.

When will we learn?

Another example of the relationship between the human and spirit realms is seen in the fact that the authority of the satanic princes listed in Daniel 10 was over geographical entities defined by humans (Persia and Greece). Whether on God's side or on Satan's, what humans do affects what happens in the spirit world, and vice-versa.

Observation 2.1
Any analysis of a given event in the human sphere needs to take into account both human and spiritual dimensions.

It is typical of Westerners, including westernized Christians, to evaluate the significant events of their lives totally at the human level, as if no supernatural activity were involved. Whether it is war, arguments in families, accidents, or natural disasters, analyzing events only on the human level is to miss the equally important supernatural dimension.

The author of a *Time* magazine cover story (May 16, 1994), that dealt with the 1994 Rwandan massacres inadvertently revealed the fact that there was a spiritual dimension to the massacres, though we doubt that the writer of the article realized the real significance of his observation. He quoted Daniel Bellamy of the United Nations High Commission for Refugees concerning the young men of the Hutu death squads: "If you look in their eyes, there is something there that is not in the eyes of normal people."[1] Concerning the same event, a missionary observed, "There are no devils left in hell. They are all in Rwanda." Each of these remarks takes note of the fact that there is a spiritual dimension as well as a human dimension to such atrocities.

A similar, though relatively unknown event took place on December 13, 1937, when the Japanese army invaded the Chinese city of Nanking in what is now referred to as "The Rape of Nanking." In the seven weeks after the invasion it is estimated that between 260,000 to 355,000 people were murdered by the Japanese soldiers before the killing began to recede. Almost all of the female victims were brutally gang-raped before being killed.

A young Japanese lieutenant named Taming Shoos reported that his men "had evil eyes. They weren't human eyes, but the eyes of leopards or tigers."[2] Looking back on his experience, he wrote, "We made them like this. Good sons, good daddies, good elder brothers at home were brought to the front to kill each other. Human beings turned into murdering demons. Everyone became a demon within three months."[3]

Another soldier, Nagatomi Hakudo, confessed, "Few know that soldiers impaled babies on bayonets and tossed them still alive into pots of boiling water. ... They gang-raped women from the ages of twelve to eighty and then killed them when they could no longer satisfy sexual requirements. I beheaded people, starved them to death, burned them, and buried them alive, over two hundred in all. It is terrible that I could turn into an animal and do these things. There are really no words to explain what I was doing. I was truly a devil."[4]

As in Rwanda, the Rape of Nanking was indeed an orgy of evil. But these are more than cases of man's inhumanity to man. They involved the cooperation of human beings with the satanic kingdom. To try to understand either Rwanda or Nanking without understanding the spiritual dimension of these events leads to misanalysis. Both human and spiritual dimensions need to be recognized and taken into account for full understanding.

In extreme events such as Rwanda and Nanking, the need

for analysis at both levels is easier to demonstrate than in lesser events such as the variety of temptations we all face or in criminal activity, deaths, and suicides.

We also hold that the spirit world is actively working with humans in positive events. When people turn to Christ, resist temptation, avoid accidents, experience blessings, receive healing, develop healthy relationships, etc., we believe there is a spiritual and human component at work. Though an understanding of human motivations, decisions and actions is crucial to analyzing an event, so is an understanding of the activities of spirit beings that relate to it. An analysis is incomplete if it does not deal with both sets of factors.

This fact challenges the western worldview. Westerners are in the habit of looking for a single cause for every event. When there is an automobile accident, for example, Westerners expect to find that it was caused by drunkenness, carelessness, fatigue, or some mechanical problem. Our perspective, however, looks for a spiritual and human cause for any given situation, or, at least, pressures coming from the spirit realm.

Observation 2.2
The principles governing the relationship between the human world and the spirit world seem to be essentially the same for both kingdoms.

God has made rules that govern the interaction between spirit and human realms, rules that both He and Satan must obey. As in the physical world there are "laws" such as gravity, the laws of chemistry and the like, so there are laws in the spirit world. While it is a contradiction, we also know that God occasionally chooses to break His own natural laws (e.g., Jesus walking on the water, multiplying the loaves and fishes, or other events we call miracles). But it is clear that He ordinarily obeys His laws and requires Satan to do likewise.

We will find several illustrations of this observation under Principle 4 below, since the rules flow largely from allegiance and obedience. Our allegiance and obedience to God, for example, gives Him greater rights to work in our affairs. On the other hand, those who commit themselves to Satan (consciously or unconsciously) and obey his commands give him opportunity to work in their lives. The same rule applies to both God and Satan and, just as with the law of gravity, it works whether or not we know of or believe in it.

Observation 2.3
The choices made by human beings affect their relationships with God and Satan.

When we obey God's laws, His power and authority are released in our lives. When we live by God's planned order as revealed in Scripture, we are positioned to receive His favor and blessing in our lives. While this doesn't spare us the tragedies life throws at us, it does position us on the receiving end of God's mercies. But when we choose to be obedient to Satan's call to stand in opposition to God's law, his dark power is released in and through us, and we become instruments of darkness.

While it has always been biblical truth and practice for Christians, it is interesting that secular psychologists are now beginning to study the effect of forgiveness on the overall mental health of a person. They are discovering that people who were able to forgive those who hurt or offended them in some way experience a literal, measurable physiological change in their body that results in a sense of relaxation and well-being. Conversely, people who are unwilling to forgive those who hurt them, retained a higher state of tension and anxiety. "Forgiveness is good for us" is the conclusion being reached. We know from Scripture that forgiveness affects our relationship with God and others. Apparently it also enhances our health.

Observation 2.4
In the human realm, God has limited His ability to protect us against evil.

We are often questioned in our deep healing prayer ministry as to why God allowed terrible, evil things to happen to people, especially innocent, defenseless children. This question often springs from humanly justified, and at times, intense anger toward God.

This "Why?" question is difficult to answer to anyone's satisfaction, especially when the questioner assumes that God has no limitations on His power. If God has no limitations and He allowed the abuse, we reason that He must not love us. Somehow, in the midst of our pain, we lose sight of the fact that God has made rules for Himself.

The most troublesome of these rules relate to God's granting of free will to us as humans. We wish that He would retract free will from those serving Satan, but He does not. Instead, He gives free will even to those who use it foolishly. And, by so giving, He places limits on Himself.

At the root of God's granting such autonomy to humans is His desire to create a being with whom to have a relationship, "to walk with and talk with in the cool of the evening" (Gen. 3:8). God desires intimacy with the men and women

He creates.

Intimacy is the desire to be fully known and accepted by another person. It is the cry of our human heart, a spiritual hunger placed there by God to draw us to Him. But God can only have intimacy with those who want intimacy with Him. He does not want clones or robots that mechanically seek and worship Him. So He creates beings with the ability to choose or reject intimacy with Him. Those who reject Him provide Satan the opportunity to deceive them into misusing their freedom to hurt others.

The rules established by the Father seem to allow every kind of abuse to occur. Yet this is not because God doesn't care or because He approves of the abuse, but rather because He is committed to honoring His own rules and, thus, respecting the free will of the perpetrator. People get abused, not because God doesn't care about them, but because someone else exercised free will and chose evil over good.

When ministering to those who are perplexed by God's apparent unwillingness to prevent their abuse, we try to help them to experience Jesus' presence in the abusive situation. They usually are able to picture Jesus in the situation as agonizing over their pain and also experiencing the abuse with them. They may even recognize that because He was there, the abuse wasn't as bad as it could have been. This process usually proves very healing, since it enables the person both to forgive God for His rules that allowed them to be hurt and to give his or her pain to Jesus.

Whatever God may allow or not allow, has nothing to do with His great love for us. God's thoughts concerning us are precious and are innumerable (Ps. 139:17). His foreknowledge does not equal His plan for us. What God does know is that He can turn whatever is meant for evil towards us into ultimate good (Rom. 8:28).

Observation 2.5
The effects of a commitment or dedication of a human being to God or Satan are carried down generationally through that person's descendants.

There seems to be a mystical relationship between members of the same family that results in children or grandchildren to at least the third or fourth generation (Ex. 20:5, 6) participating in or experiencing the results of commitments made by their ancestors. God speaks of this in the Ten Commandments stating that He will punish the descendents of those who commit themselves to the enemy down to the third and fourth generation, but bless the descendants of those who love Him down through thousands of generations (Ex. 20:5, 6).

This principle is illustrated many times in Scripture. God's love for and faithfulness to generations of Israelites, stemming from Abraham's commitment to Him is the most prominent of these scriptural illustrations. Elsewhere, we see David's faithfulness to God brought divine blessing to Solomon and to Solomon's descendants (I Kings 11:34-36), despite the fact that Solomon and his descendants were unfaithful to the Lord. In II Kings 8:19 we read, "The Lord was not willing to destroy Judah, because He had promised His servant David that his descendants would always continue to rule." This they did until the fall of Jerusalem reported in II Kings 25.

On the negative side, Adam's disobedience brought the curse of God on all generations (Gen. 3:17-19). On a smaller scale David curses Joab and his descendants for his treacherous murder of Abner (II Sam. 3:28-29).

We find over and over again in ministry sessions that strong demons inhabit the children and grandchildren of persons who have committed themselves to or who have been dedicated to the gods (demons) of non-Christian religions. We also find demons in the descendants of those who belonged to occult organizations such as Freemasonry, Scientology, Mormonism, Jehovah's Witnesses, and the like.

Observation 2.6
Through our allegiance to God or Satan, spirit beings gain influence for the expression of power and control in the lives of human beings.

When we worship God, we are exercising our will to invite God to be the spiritual center of our lives. By doing so we position ourselves spiritually for the release of God's power and influence in our lives through the Holy Spirit.

The same is true on the other side. Any act of dedication to, or worship of, anything or anyone other than God invites Satan to work in our lives. When people seek the spiritual power or "enlightenment" offered through various Eastern religions, New Age teachings, Freemasonry, Scientology, or the like they open themselves up to God's enemy. Even if the person is naive and the commitment marginal or even just done in jest, what they actually are doing is pledging allegiance to the power behind that religion or organization. This allegiance gives Satan specific rights to them.

When New Agers or persons in Eastern religions seek "spirit guides," they actually are inviting demons to be their teachers without knowing it. The seduction is that the demons will actually be benevolent for a season to draw the person into the worship of darkness, parading their "hidden knowledge" as the "true" path to enlightenment. Others are seduced into darkness because they were told that the rituals they were performing and the vows they were making were merely "fun and games" (e.g., the blood oaths men take upon entering the Masonic Order). They were not, however, told that Satan takes these oaths very seriously and these oaths give demons the right to inhabit those who make the oaths.

Observation 2.7
The rights given by people to spirit powers extend to people's property and territory.

People attuned to the Spirit of God need only to walk into a pagan temple anywhere in the world to sense the spiritual darkness there. Pagan temples, New Age churches, meeting places of cults, occult bookstores, idol shrines, and places of Satanic worship all emanate a feeling of demonic presence.

Even a hotel room can house spirits that were drawn by previous evil activity in that room. We routinely suggest that upon entering a hotel room, one dedicate it to Christ and command anything belonging to the enemy to leave it immediately. We then ask Jesus to fill the room with angels who will protect us while we dwell there. Spiritual cleansing and sealing the television set is recommended too because of the spirits that may have entered into that room through the watching of horror, violent, or pornographic movies. Even though we do not own the room, we have rented it and, therefore, have legal rights over it. Hence we have to spiritually cleanse the room.

A case in point, one woman we know called her husband once while on a business trip to New York City and mentioned that sexual thoughts were going through her mind that she normally would never entertain. After further discussion the husband reminded her that she had forgotten to take spiritual authority over the room. Once this was done, the thoughts immediately stopped. The sexual spirit in the room had been ordered out!

On the positive side, when people serve God, that allegiance "spills over" to their possessions, their houses and their lands. In II Chronicles 7:14, repentance resulted in the land of God's people being made prosperous again. Even though there is this "spill over" effect, we suggest that those who buy or rent property use the authority of Christ to cleanse the property from whatever might have happened on it in the past, including repentance for any sin committed on the property since a detailed history of the land and house is usually not known

The "Transformations" video recently produced by the Sentinel Group (George Otis, Jr.) talks of a city in Latin America where a large number of the residents repented of their evil deeds and turned to Christ. Since that time, the produce in this agricultural community has greatly flourished. God literally "healed" their land in response to their repentance. It might also be that their repentance broke some demonic bondage over their land, freeing it to flourish.[5]

A couple we know once bought a home knowing full well that the previous owners were involved in a New Age cult and that Hare Krishna priests had been invited onto the land. Prior to knowing about the need to spiritually clean the house and land and dedicate it to God, the wife was often awakened at night by the presence of a dark figure in the master bedroom. It manifested itself to her in the appearance of a mummy, and called itself the Black Man. This spirit later revealed that it had the right to be in the bedroom because the former owner's wife had invited him to dwell there. (We believe he was some form of "spirit guide" she had invited to serve her.) The Lord revealed to her husband that as the new owner of the land he was to walk the perimeter of the lot dedicating it to the Lord. At each corner of the lot he was to drive a stake into the ground that had been anointed with oil, declaring to the heavens that the land marked by the stakes belonged to Jesus. After this was done the dark figure appeared to the wife two more times. But each time, a hastily awakened husband authoritatively reminded the spirit that it had no more rights to the property and commanded it to leave immediately. After the second appearance, the Black Man spirit was seen no more.

Other examples of this observation include a demon we once cast out of a woman who claimed the right to inhabit her because she lived in a house where a previous occupant had committed adultery. Only when we claimed her authority as the new owner of the property were we able to break the power granted the demon by the previous owner and to cast it out.

We have also dealt with demons that appeared to have rights to a home through previous occult activity in it and a demon that claimed rights through a death that occurred in the home. On another occasion, a demon claimed rights to a church due to the sin of adultery that had been committed in the church by a former pastor.

Notes

1. Nancy Gibbs, "Why? The Killing Fields of Rwanda," *Time*, May 16, 1994, Vol. 143, No. 20.
2. Iris Chang, *The Rape of Nanking* (New York, NY: Penguin Books, 1998), p. 57.
3. Ibid., p. 58
4. Ibid., p. 59
5. "Transformations," video hosted by George Otis, Jr., The Sentinel Group, 1999.

CHAPTER FIVE

———◆———

Principle Three:
There Are Certain Major Differences
Between How God and
Satan Operate

While there are similarities in the ways that God and Satan operate within the human and spiritual realms, there are also distinct differences. This chapter highlights the fact that although a specific principle applies to both kingdoms, it is carried out in diametrically different ways.

Observation 3.1
God works with integrity; Satan works
by deception.

God is a God of truth. He gains our allegiance by straightforwardly and lovingly telling us the terms of His "contract" with us. He never misleads us, makes promises He does not intend to keep or offers us things that He does not intend to give us. His terms in the "contract" are clear. He offers things such as salvation and eternal life (John 5:24), a place in His family

(John 1:12), and peace and rest (Matt. 11:28). He also states honestly that following His way will result in disfavor with, and even persecution from, nonbelievers (John 15:18-21). Yet obedience results in Divine blessing; disobedience results in Divine judgment and punishment. His character demands that He fulfill His promises to us, if we fulfill our part of the contract.

Satan, on the other hand, usually gains allegiance through deceit and deception. He draws persons into his kingdom through promises he doesn't intend to keep, as he did with Eve in the Garden (Gen. 3:5). He may use deceptive fronts such as New Age teachings or harmless looking, but occult-oriented devices like, Ouija Boards and Tarot cards. The present popularity among young people of occultic and violent video games is a deceptive plan of the enemy to draw these unsuspecting young people into the world of evil. Satan also seduces persons into his kingdom through participation in occult groups that parade as service groups (Freemasonry, fortune tellers) or religions (Mormonism, Islam, Buddhism, Scientology, The New Age). Though Satan can disguise himself as an angel of light (II Cor. 11:14), his real intention is to steal, kill, and destroy (John 10:10).

We once worked with a woman who had been involved in the New Age Movement for many years. She told us of the increased knowledge and power she was receiving as long as she served the "spirit guides" and followed her guru's instructions, including his use of her sexually. She had become a much sought after teacher in New Age circles, having gained much knowledge and power from her "guides." But just at the time she thought she was finally arriving at "enlightenment," she suddenly found herself totally abandoned by her "spirits." This situation cast her into a deep despair that took her to the edge of suicide. Fortunately, Jesus was able to break through her darkness and bring her into the Light.

Observation 3.2
God leads His followers to freedom; Satan leads his followers into captivity.

A spiritual power can give to its followers only what it owns. Paul says that obedience to Satan is enslavement to sin, whereas obedience to God brings freedom from sin and, if we receive it, the gift eternal life (Rom. 6:16-18, 22-23). Satan owns death and waits to give it to those who follow him, though he seldom advertises this in his initial "sales pitch" or temptation. God, on the other hand, is eternal life and waits to give it to those who follow Him. Satan can only give his followers the fruits of sin (things such as rebellion, deceit, anger, and lust), perversions of the potentially good qualities that God built into human beings. He has nothing else to offer. Ultimately, all of Satan's gifts, whether they are spiritual or physical, lead to death. Moreover, none of his gifts are eternal, except hell. God, on the other hand, can give us freedom from the hindrances of sin, enable us to become all that He has created us to be and bless us with His gifts, including eternal life.

Observation 3.3
God inhabits His people with His Holy Spirit. The best Satan can do is inhabit his people with some of his angels, called demons.

This observation highlights an incredible difference between the work of God and the work of Satan. The best Satan can do is indwell those who give allegiance to him with some of his angel-level demons. Even if Satan himself were to indwell someone, that person would still only be visited by an angelic being, albeit a powerful one. God on the other hand, inhabits us with Himself in the person of the Holy Spirit. He becomes the source of our strength and power. And when we do battle with the enemy, it is the Holy Spirit in us who leads the way. One can only be left to ponder why people would choose allegiance to Satan over an indwelling by the Eternal God. But such is the nature of deception and evil that it clouds our discernment and perverts our choices.

Observation 3.4
Satan can use God's laws and biblical principles to accomplish his purposes in the human realm.

A good example of how Satan perverts God's laws and principles is seen in the spiritual dynamic identified by John and Paula Sandford which they have labeled "bitter root judgments."[1] This designation grew out of their observation that people often repeat in their own lives the very things that they judged in their parents' lives. The Sandford's hunch was that there was a spiritual principle at work that caused this to happen. How else could they explain people who became or did the very thing they judged in their parents? Although this principle is not clearly identified in Scripture, it reflects biblical and experiential truth. The descriptive name came from Hebrews 12:15, "See to it that no one misses the grace of God, and that no bitter root grows up to cause trouble and defile many."

The dynamics of the bitter root judgment is that the enemy takes the judgments (legitimate and illegitimate) we make against our parents (and other parental figures) and supernaturally empowers them so that we reproduce and repeat in our lives the very things we judged in our parents' lives. Like the martial arts principle of using your opponent's size and strength against him, a bitter root judgment counterfeits God's biblical principles (our strength as believers) and uses them to bring bondage and destruction in our lives (the bitter root judgment). The bitter root judgment is fueled by four spiritual principles created by God to bless us, but perverted by Satan to enslave us:

1. The first spiritual principle Satan uses to form bitter root judgments is a commandment: "Honor your father and your mother, so that you may live long in the land the Lord your God is giving you" (Ex. 20:12).

2. The second spiritual principle Satan uses in forming the bitter root judgment is "the principle of sowing and reaping." It is stated in Galatians 6:7, "Do not be deceived: God cannot be mocked. A man reaps what he sows." In the spiritual realm, whatever we sow, we receive back, and often in greater proportions. We sow a watermelon seed, and we get a watermelon back. Whatever we do, good or bad, will pay dividends, good or bad.

3. The third spiritual principle at work in bitter root judgments concerns judging others. Jesus laid down this principle in the Sermon on the Mount: "Do not judge, or you too will be judged. For in the same way you judge others, you will be judged, and with the measure you use, it will be measured to you" (Matt. 7:1-2).

4. The fourth spiritual principle focuses on those who have offended us. Again, this principle comes from the Sermon on the Mount: "For if you forgive men when they sin

against you, your heavenly Father will also forgive you. But if you do not forgive men their sins, your father will not forgive your sins" (Matt. 6:14-15).

Each of these principles is grounded in a strong, biblical truth that, if followed, brings good fruit into our lives. But, because Satan desires to subvert the intentions of God, he uses the spiritual power of these four God-created principles against us by weaving them into a twisted bitter root judgment principle that he then releases into our lives.

Essentially, a bitter root judgment occurs when Satan takes the judgments we make against our parents and/or parental figures and empowers them with demonic power to cause us to create and bring about in our lives the very things we judged in our parents' lives. We have encountered this spiritual bondage repeatedly in people who have come to us for help. Sadly, their lives exemplify how Satan perverts the principles of God for his own purposes.

The good news is that God our Father can undo whatever Satan does. The Sandford's use family and personal history and words of knowledge to identify these judgments and then have the person renounce and repent for having made them. The Father has shown us a different approach that works effectively in our ministry model. In a ministry session, we ask the Holy Spirit to reveal to the person in prayer all of the unanswered questions in the heart of the child within them—questions the child never asked (but thought about) or questions the child asked, but were never answered. We believe the enemy translates these unanswered questions in the child into bitter root judgments.

As the Holy Spirit reveals these unanswered questions to the person we guide them to verbally ask the questions the Holy Spirit is showing them and we write them down. When the "inner child who was wounded" is finished asking all their unanswered questions, we then go back and have them renounce these judgments one at a time in the name of Jesus. This simple act of renunciation nullifies the demonic power that has held the person captive and invalidates the right of the enemy to reap bad fruit in their life through bitter root judgments. After renouncing these judgments, persons usually report a changed attitude toward their parents and often find it easier to relate to their parents, even ones of the "evil" variety. There also seems to be a new freedom released in the person to begin to correct their own behavior patterns traced to the bitter root judgments against their parents.

In ministry sessions dealing with bitter root judgments people have identified as few as three or four and as many as 150 judgments toward an abusive parent. Again, bitter root judgments are a good example of how Satan uses God's principles and laws to his advantage.

Observation 3.5
Those committed to God adopt the character of God; those committed to Satan adopt the character of Satan.

The character of the King shapes His Kingdom. God's people are called to reflect His character, though it is done imperfectly because of their sin nature. They know the Father's voice and, if not in rebellion, seek to follow it. Commitment to God results in righteousness, peace, and love. Those who do not choose God, either intentionally or by default, align themselves with Satan. They usually reflect the character of deception, pride, envy, deceit, and evil that characterizes their leader, Satan.

Observation 3.6
God can be trusted; Satan cannot.

God's very character personifies righteousness, truth, and justice. Because He cannot be other than He is, God is utterly trustworthy. Satan also cannot be anything but what he is. The dishonest, deceitful character of the enemy means that we cannot trust anything he says or does. Common sense dictates that we should never trust a liar. The devil, by character, is a liar (John 8:44) and a thief (John 10:10), and so cannot be trusted, ever! So it is a paradox that people routinely believe what he says.

Satan offers his followers things that only God can give, such as happiness, comfort, power, success, and love. But in reality, he only offers these items long enough to ensnare and enslave a person in his darkness. Satan even has the power to do counterfeit miracles and certain signs and wonders, like Pharaoh's magicians did. But these counterfeits don't last either (Ex. 7:10-13). Paul called this ability "counterfeit miracles, signs and wonders" (II Thes. 2:9-10). Satan's whole kingdom is counterfeit because it is based on "borrowed power," broken promises and false claims. On the other hand, what God promises He will do, He will do.

Observation 3.7
God offers the genuine; Satan can only counterfeit.

Satan, masquerading as one of God's angels (II Cor. 11:14), is able to counterfeit much of what only God can give. This may occur during the New Age practice of inviting "spirit guides" to come and dispense "the wisdom of the ages." Whereas God sends the Holy Spirit as the teacher of Truth, Satan sends his dark agents as false teachers of "light." Since Satan has no creative power, he must use his delegated power to copy and counterfeit the signs and wonders of God, as in the case of Pharaoh's magicians with Moses mentioned above. Only God can offer genuine things that last, that have no "shelf life," so to speak, such as genuine peace, joy, power, and the ability to do freeing signs and wonders. Satan's gifts seem to come with an "expiration date" attached.

Even Satan's kingdom is a counterfeit kingdom. His kingdom is buttressed by deceit in place of truth, the delegated power of a rebellious archangel in place of the power that comes from the true source, false promises in place of honesty, blessings that turn into curses, darkness in place of light, and death in place of life.

Observation 3.8
God offers us a "true self" while Satan offers us a "false self."

We have observed in human relationships, especially in the marriage arena, that people seem to believe that "the best defense is a good offense"—when one is wrong, attack the other person, putting him or her on the defensive. Such behavior is a manifestation of our sin nature and an expression of what may be called our "false self." It is part of Satan's strategy to keep our "true self" hidden from us.

Our true self is the essence of life within us imprinted by the hand of God. The true self declares whom we are before God—our worth, our value and what the Father sees in us. When we see our true self clearly, we are freed to be who the

Father created us to be—salt and light in a world of sin and darkness. Hence, the fierce determination of Satan to keep this true self from us.

The strategy behind this evil agenda is easily understood. Satan must wound our hearts as early as possible and wound them in such ways that they cannot receive the messages of God's truth. He must get to the true self implanted within our hearts at conception and replace it with the false self—a self that reflects what Satan says about us and which he wants us to come to accept as our own view of ourselves. He does this through evil. Evil is when the hand of Satan touches the heart of humankind with the intention of destroying the purposes of God.

The result of this touch by evil is the creation of the false self—a damaged image of ourselves grounded in the lies, deceptions, pains, and distortions created from our personal woundedness by Satan. Once this false self is created and implanted in our hearts, Satan's strategy then becomes to constantly hold this false image before our eyes, continuing to reinterpret it and apply it to all the continuing events of our lives. In a sense, we are then constantly looking at God and life through Satan's filters. We are unable to see the true image of ourselves implanted by God. Instead, our focus, through our pain, is constantly on what Satan says about us, instead of what Father God says about us.

Fortunately for us, Jesus' death on the Cross destroyed the power of Satan and his ability to hold us in this deception. Jesus' Cross shouts at us our worth and value to a loving Heavenly Father. The fact that so many can't see it illustrates Satan's success in getting us to believe his lies. Much of our success in prayer ministry comes as we begin to help people reject and renounce the lies Satan has spoken into their hearts so they can affirm the reality of what God says about them.

Observation 3.9
God can override His rules for Creation; Satan cannot override God's rules.

God created certain rules that govern the interaction of the spiritual world and the natural world. It is our belief that these are rules that even He has chosen to abide by, even in the face of His children being destroyed by evil. But, for reasons known only to God, occasionally it appears that God can and does override His own rules to do something out of the natural order of things. Whether it is superceding a natural law like gravity in the parting of the Red Sea (Ex. 14:15-31), the law of combustion in the incident of the Burning Bush (Ex. 3-4:17), or a law of the universe on the day the sun stood still (Josh. 10:12-14), or a law of physical process like healing a withered hand (Mark 3:1-6), God has the ability to set aside the very rules He established in Creation to accomplish His purposes.

When God does choose to violate the rules He has established, regardless of their category, it falls into the category we call "signs and wonders" or "miracles" spoken of in Scripture. These are times when God supernaturally imposes His will to override the natural laws of the universe to accomplish His purposes. He can even choose to work outside the "ground rules" presented in this book.

While God has the ability to do this, Satan does not. He must operate within the rules and laws the Father established. It appears that he can only operate outside those laws by permission of the Father, as in the case of Job and the harsh tragedies that befell him. The Father, on the other hand, can set aside the rules as He deems necessary out of His extravagant love for us. But this seems to occur only in special cases we call "signs and wonders and miracles," and is not the normal process He follows. As a rule, God follows His rules.

Notes

1. John and Paula Sandford, *The Transformation of the Inner Man* (South Plainfield, NJ: Bridge, 1982), pp. 237-266.

CHAPTER SIX

PRINCIPLE FOUR:
The Obtaining and Exercising of Spiritual Power and Authority By Humans Flow From Allegiance, Relationship, and Obedience to Either God or Satan

Humans can receive empowerment from either God or Satan. Jesus gave His authority to His disciples, an authority that included authority over demons and disease, while He was still on earth (Luke 9:1-2). After His ascension, Jesus promised and then sent the Holy Spirit to continue to empower His followers to do even greater works than He did (John 14:12). But that authority was given in the context of a relationship—the relationship of Jesus with His followers.

The same process works in the satanic kingdom (see Observation 1.1). Satan promises power to those who will give him their allegiance and serve him. That is the whole basis and purpose of satanic worship and rituals. The cult members are promised increasing levels of personal power and strength as a result of obedience to Satan. What most cultists don't realize is that Satan is very unpredictable and does not always deliver on his promises (see Observation 3.5).

In either kingdom, God's or Satan's, a basic requirement for humans to legitimately receive and exercise the authority of their leader is a relationship with the leader based on allegiance and obedience. Though the apostles regularly cast out demons on the authority flowing from their relationship with Jesus, the sons of Sceva attempted to exercise that same authority without the proper relationship with Jesus and were made to pay for their mistake (Acts 19:13-16).

Observation 4.1
God and Satan can invest people, places, and things with power.

Allegiance and obedience are the conduits of power, whether the power is coming from God or from Satan. A significant difference is that when the investing comes from God, it is through the indwelling of the Holy Spirit. Each believer gets the same Holy Spirit. Though individual Christians may have different spiritual giftings, they all have the same authority, the authority of Jesus given to His followers (John 14:12-13).

In contrast to this, the amount of power and authority Satan's followers have depends on their status in Satan's kingdom. Their ranking is revealed by the strength of the demons they have invited into themselves or that they have been given for their service to the kingdom of darkness. The greater their acts of evil, the greater their strength and their responsiveness to the control of the demons.

In the same way, places and things can be spiritually empowered through being dedicated to God or Satan, or through their frequent use in the service of that power (e.g. pagan temples, places of worship, places of prayer, idol shrines, Masonic and Mormon temples, adult book stores). Objects dedicated to, or used in the worship of, God or Satan can also be empowered. Crosses, crucifixes, idols, and voodoo masks are all objects used in worship to a power, and draw their power from that power. It is interesting to watch how demons react to being confronted with a cross during deliverance. They understand the symbol and the power attached to it.

It amazes us how many Christians who travel or live in foreign countries bring back dedicated artifacts and relics and keep them in their homes or offices as souvenirs. They have no clue about the demonic power center they have brought into their lives. We once visited the headquarters of a large international Christian relief agency. As we walked the halls and looked in offices, we were astounded to see all of the pagan masks, idols, and religious paraphernalia hanging on walls and sitting on shelves as remembrances of trips abroad by staff members. We wonder if some of the confusion and interoffice conflict and tensions in that organization can be traced to the activity of spirits attached to these pagan objects.

What most people do not realize is that it is customary in many societies for such objects to be dedicated to evil spirits, even if they do not serve specifically religious purposes. While such demonized objects can be cleansed in the authority of Jesus, most Christians don't realize the need to do this, so it is never done. If you have any such things in your possession, we encourage you to at least claim the authority of Jesus to cancel any enemy power attached to them and to bless them with the power and authority of Jesus.

If the objects have a specifically religious purpose, or if you notice bad things happening in your life that you suspect are related to these objects, it is our recommendation that you dispose of them altogether.

Scriptural illustrations of empowerment by God include the Ark of the Covenant (I Sam 4-7), the Temple, Jesus' garments (Matt. 9:20) and Paul's handkerchiefs and aprons (Acts 19:11-12). Satan's power is invested in idols, cups, and tables of demons (I Cor. 10:21) and even doctrine (I Tim 4:1).

Observation 4.2

There are certain limitations to what God and Satan can do in the human realm. These limitations are related to the cooperation God and Satan receive from humans.

Neither God nor Satan can get their way all the time. The issue of the free will of the individual is always the deciding factor. Both God and Satan seek our allegiance directly and work in and through circumstances and other people to influence us in our choices. There is an eternal competition for our allegiance, both kingdoms trying to draw us to their side, and at the same time trying to keep us from the other side. Satan's workings are frequently frustrated when people cooperate with God, and vice-versa. The difference in the competition is that God attempts to woo us with truth while Satan tries to draw us into his camp with deception (see Observation 3:1). God tells us the truth about ourselves and about Satan; Satan tells us lies about ourselves and about God (see Observation 3:7).

Contrary to some theologies, God does not always get His way. For example, we know that He doesn't want anyone to go to hell (II Peter 3:9), but many will. This is a part of Satan's plan that is succeeding. Satan's primary desire is to thwart God's plans through keeping people from committing their lives to God or by tempting God's people to disobey Him or to neglect their relationship with Him. He does this most effectively through either keeping people ignorant of what God desires (II Cor. 4:4), or by deceiving them into disobeying God (Gen. 3:1-7).

But, God also frequently frustrates Satan's plans through gaining the obedience of people who convert to Christ and serve Him faithfully in the Body of Believers. In deliverance sessions we have encountered many frustrated demons whose main complaint was that they could not get the person in whom they lived to do what the demon wanted them to do. The usual reason given by the demon for this frustration is that the person is too busy serving God. One spirit of lust in a man complained to us, "I can't get him to look at women anymore!" Another complained about a woman, "She spends too much time reading that Bible. I can't get her to listen to me anymore!"

Observation 4.3
To accomplish their purposes, God and Satan ordinarily work in the human realm through partnerships with humans.

God and Satan accomplish their purposes in the human realm most successfully and purposefully when they are working in tandem with humans. In fact, often is the case where their objectives could not be accomplished until they had human cooperation. Because he lived in fellowship with God when no one else did, Noah was called by God to build an ark. But, Noah had to be willing to do something that made no practical sense to anyone. He did it because God told him to and by his obedience saved himself and his family from the flood (Gen. 6-10). The Children of Israel could not come into existence until a man named Abram was willing to partner with God and to leave polytheism and the land of his father to go and worship the one true God in the land of Canaan (Gen. 12:1-9).

Satan got Joseph's brothers to partner with him to sell Joseph into slavery in Egypt, but God partnered with Joseph to save the Israelites from famine because of his faithfulness to God (Gen. 50:19-20). The Israelites prospered in Egypt because of Joseph, until Satan could get a Pharaoh to partner with him to break the agreement made hundreds of years earlier between the Egyptians and Israelites. Satan used this Pharaoh's fear of the sheer numbers of the Israelites in Egypt to get him to put them into slavery (Ex. 1:1-11). Then Moses was called by God to partner with Him to go and set His people free. He obeyed and eventually led God's people out of bondage in Egypt (Ex. 3:1-21).

Concerning the birth of Jesus, God partnered with Joseph and Mary to bring Jesus into the world. Then Satan partnered with Herod to try to kill Jesus before He could grow up, whereupon God and Joseph partnered again to take the baby to Egypt to save His life. Then, of course, Jesus as a human being partnered with God to carry out the plan of salvation that results in our redemption.

Throughout human history, this fact of partnership has repeated itself. God and Satan can work their separate plans, but each usually has to have human partnership to be successful. A current application of this principle is our experience with inner healing and deliverance ministry with a person. While we are there leading the ministry session, it is the Holy Spirit working in partnership with us that brings healing and spiritual freedom. In fact, we routinely declare to the demonic spirits present that we have no authority or power of our own, but that we work in and through the power of Jesus and the Holy Spirit. This is partnership at its best!

Observation 4.4
Through human allegiance and obedience, God and Satan gain legal rights to work in human affairs.

Whenever we choose light over darkness, we release God to have more ability to do what He wants to do in our lives. When we choose darkness, we release Satan to have more authority to do what he wants to do in our lives.

On God's side, obedience to His rules, including such things as committing ourselves to Christ, praying, worshipping, being righteous, loving others, confessing sin, and the like releases God's power and enables Him to do what He seeks to do both within and through us. On Satan's side, disobeying God by sinning, not forgiving, hating, committing oneself to Satan, seeking help from him, worshiping him in cultic rituals, being unrighteous, or the like releases Satan's power and enables him to do his work in and through us.

As long as Adam was obedient, God could work in and through him in the world. But when Adam chose to listen to Satan's voice, God lost His ability to work through Adam, and Satan gained the right to infect Adam and all his descendents with sin. Satan was also able to usurp the authority to have dominion over the world that had been given to Adam by God (Luke 4:6).

An example of how our choices affect the strategies of God and Satan is seen in Numbers 13-14. God's plan for the people to enter the Promised Land had to be revised when the people refused His order to cross over at Kadesh. God was prepared to destroy His people for their rebellion, but Moses appealed to God's reputation among the Egyptians and God reconsidered His decision. He chose to not destroy the children of Israel, but He did say that no one who had rebelled against Him above twenty years of age would live to cross the Jordan River and see the Promised Land. Of the original group that escaped Egypt, only Caleb and Joshua lived to cross the Jordan River forty years later and possess the land God had promised to Abraham. God was eventually able to bring His people into the Promised Land by instituting "Plan B" (or Plan C or Plan D). One can only wonder what the history of Israel (and our history) would have been had they crossed the Jordan and taken the land the first time!

The same rules still apply to us as the literal and symbolic descendents of Abraham. Obedience to God releases God's power in and through us. Obedience to Satan's voice releases Satan's power in and through us. The key is always our choice, since neither God nor Satan can violate our will.

Likewise, when God seeks to enter a person's life, it won't happen until the person invites Him in. When people don't obey God by praying and witnessing, people are lost, in spite of the fact that it is not God's will that any should perish (II Peter 3:9). But it is also true that when God's people obey by praying, repenting, and turning from evil, God can forgive and bring revival (II Chron. 7:14).

When a person is disobedient either to God or to Satan, spiritually the legal rights to that person are weakened, though not necessarily broken. If a Christian sins (obeys Satan), but obediently repents quickly, the relationship with God is maintained and restored. When those who have committed themselves to Satan in occult organizations such as New Age religions or Freemasonry convert to Christ, their relationship to Satan is damaged, but not necessarily broken. The reason we say this is that the demons they invited in while active in such things still live inside them and exercise considerable influence. Complete freedom comes only as these intruders are identified and cast out.

Observation 4.5
Rituals such as sacrifice, worship, and prayer seem to enable God or Satan.

In such activities we Christians express our obedience to God and our partnership with Him. These are acts of war in which we line up our wills with the will of our Leader to accomplish what He desires. Those who follow Satan, then, line up their wills with his in the same way. We will deal with ritual and sacrifice other than blood sacrifice here and treat blood sacrifice in the next observation (4.6).

Prayer and worship are the simplest, yet most powerful weapons we have in our arsenal. Prayer is the most easily utilized "ritual" and the one most frequently practiced throughout Scripture. Jesus regularly prayed and commanded His followers to do the same. The most notable types of prayer in Jesus' ministry were what we would call "intimacy prayer" and "authority prayer." Jesus regularly spent time alone with the Father in His practice of intimacy. On the basis of the empowerment received in those quiet moments, He was then able "do what He saw the Father doing" (John 5:19), to authoritatively teach, heal, and cast out demons. When Jesus chose His apostles, He commissioned them first for intimacy, and then for authoritative ministry (Mark 3:14).

As Christians we often tend to forget that for every church praying to God there is probably a Satanic group nearby praying to Satan, and against us! Interestingly, the two groups are praying for the same thing, but to different sources of power. Both are asking for favor and power from the source of their allegiance to thwart the success of the other group over them.

When God is the focus of our rituals of prayer, worship, and sacrifices, enemy forces have to stand back and watch because our Lord is infinitely more powerful than the devil.

As Christians we make sacrifices to God through such things as the lifestyles we choose, fasting, giving our lives in full-time service to God, celibacy, or giving sacrificial offerings above our basic tithe. We also use certain rituals in our churches to honor God and enable Him to accomplish His purposes. These include things like worship, prayers, offerings, communion services, baptism, and the like. While Evangelical churches tend to see our rituals as more symbolic, orthodox and many mainline denominational churches see them as more sacramental in nature. Our Christian rituals help release God to do in and through us what He wants to do.

Since Satan is a copier of what God does and operates according to the same rules, it is predictable that Satanists do the same things for their god as Christians do for theirs. Most anything Christians do in the service and worship of God, the followers of Satan do in the service and worship of Satan.

Observation 4.6
Through blood sacrifices, power is released to the followers of God or Satan.

Blood is representative of the essence of life. As such, it is treated and respected as a life force among all peoples. In the Levitical Laws that governed the Israelites' daily life, the instructions governing animal sacrifice and the resultant shedding of blood were very carefully delineated. Attention was even given in the Law to a woman's menstrual blood, and how she and others were to relate to it. From these early references, it is obvious that blood must have held a special significance to

God, hence all the rules governing it. Therefore, there is a powerful spiritual connection between this life force and how it is used.

In the hierarchy of Levitical Laws mentioned above, blood rituals were perceived as the most powerful. This was first seen in the practice of animal sacrifice in the early days of the Old Testament. It was dramatically portrayed in Abraham's willingness to sacrifice Isaac (Gen. 22:1-14). It was graphically portrayed in the Passover event in Egypt, where a lamb's blood painted on the doorposts of the homes of the Israelites spared them the death of their firstborn sons and firstborn animals. It is later seen in the elaborate sacrificial system of the Temple, where the shedding of an animal's blood cancelled the guilt of sin in the person offering the sacrifice.

If blood is important to God, then it must have a counterfeit meaning and application for Satan as well. This is illustrated in the earlier reference to the sacrifice of the King of Moab's son on the walls of his besieged city in II Kings 3:21-27 (see p. 40). The shedding of the blood of the king's firstborn son turned the tide of battle against Israel. The Israelites didn't bother to ask God what He could do to counteract this sacrifice. Instead, they just ran. Such was the effect of the spiritual power unleashed against them through the shedding of the boy's blood to empower the Moabite god, Chemosh.

As mentioned earlier (see p. 40), the legalization of abortion is one of the modern day ritualistic equivalents to what the King of Moab did. We cannot even begin to imagine how that has empowered Satan and his demons to new heights of evil in the current day. The fact that a high percentage of abortions are of what would have been "firstborns" only heightens the tragedy and increases the power that Satan has unleashed on an unsuspecting society that naively views abortion as a "human right," when it is actually a "human wrong."

That shed blood specifically empowers God explains why the atoning work of Christ on the Cross is of such cosmic consequence. In the Old Testament, blood was both the symbol and the empowerment of the covenant of God with His people. The very next day, after Moses told the people all the Lord's commands and the people agreed to them, he took the blood of cattle that had been sacrificed to the Lord and threw half of it on the altars. The other half of the blood he threw on the people, proclaiming as he did it, "This is the blood that seals the covenant which the Lord made with you when he gave you these commands " (Ex. 24:8).

Setting the stage for the meaning of the Cross, the writer of Hebrews reviewed Moses' actions, declaring that the first covenant "went into effect only with the use of blood" (Heb. 9:18). The writer then points us to the meaning of the Cross, when he declares, "Indeed, according to the Law almost everything is purified by blood, and sins are forgiven only if blood is poured out" (Heb. 9:22). Eugene Peterson in translating this passage in *The Message* (NavPress), calls it "the final solution to sin."

So we can see, spiritually shed blood releases power. For Christians, the shedding of Christ's blood on the Cross sealed the New Covenant God made with us. The way to God now became Christ, not blood sacrifices. The blood of Christ was the final sacrifice. Perhaps that is why blood was so important to God. He knew what it was going to mean. It was going to require that His Son die. And now our authority and spiritual power does not come from shedding more blood, but from invoking the power released by the blood of Jesus which was shed once and for all, which we regularly do in ministry sessions.

Interestingly, those who worship Satan must still shed blood to empower him. They cannot invoke the blood of Satan for power and authority, because it has none. Instead, they must shed other blood, having drawn it from an animal or human source. While many occultic and witchcraft rituals require blood of some type, in the worse cases of satanic ritual abuse, the shedding of blood actually involves the taking of a human life as a part of the ritual. The younger and more innocent the person sacrificed the better. Satanists like to sacrifice newborns and virgin girls whenever possible, perhaps to do their best to approximate in their victims the purity and guiltlessness of Jesus. The Satanists also believe the more evil they can perpetrate on these innocent victims, the more power Satan will give them in the cult.

For Christians, however, the power of blood is found in the power of the blood of Jesus, and no other. In ministry sessions we routinely invoke the power of Jesus' blood against the evil we encounter. Sometimes we call on it as a healing presence, sometimes as a cleansing presence, sometimes as a warring presence, but most often as an authority presence. Demons react negatively at the mere mention of the blood of Jesus, and most are relieved to have permission to leave when threatened with its power.

Observation 4.7
The spirit world works within the human world according to authority relationships.

Not enough can be said about the role of authority in the spiritual world. Kraft addresses this whole area more fully in his book *I Give You Authority* (Chosen Books). The demonic world is structured around authority, apparently with a hierarchy of leadership and function, as suggested in Ephesians 6:12.

In Scripture, there are numerous descriptions of authority

in the body of Christ. Husbands over wives (not boss, but leader) (Eph. 5:23, I Tim. 2:11-14), of parents over children (Eph. 6:1-3, Col. 3:20), of pastors and other leaders over the people in their churches (Eph. 4:11-12, I Tim. 3), of rulers over their people (I Tim. 2:2; Rom. 13:1-2), and older people over younger people. We also see an application of spiritual authority implied in I Corinthians 7:14 of a believing spouse to make the unbelieving spouse and their children acceptable to God. This verse should be of comfort to women married to unbelieving husbands, since it gives them authority to "sanctify" both husband and children.

In a similar way, when people put themselves under the authority of spirit guides (demons), cult leaders, or a false religion, many of God's limitations on Satan's activities are removed. We even question the real intent behind many of the occult-themed video games popular with young people. While not paranoid, we do suspect the motive behind the rash of these games is more than profit. We have encountered demons that gained access to a person through their absorption into an occult-oriented video game to the point that they lost touch with their own reality and took on the reality of the game. While they could re-enter their own reality later, by then the demonic damage had been done. The same dynamic is accomplished through the constant involvement in occult-oriented music, such as Gothic music.

Demons operate according to authority relationships. In deliverance, our motto is to "follow the fruit to the root." We first seek to address the recurring sin or areas of weakness in a person through inner healing prayer. We then challenge and dispose of the demon in the person assigned to push that area of sin or temptation in the person's thought process. In our deliverance model, which is documented in Charles Kraft's book, *Defeating Dark Angels* (Servant Publications), we are always looking for a demonic authority structure or hierarchy in a person. Our goal in identifying this structure is to get to the top of the one or more demonic authority chains in the person, to what we refer to as the "head spirit" of each group in the body.

Those in spiritual authority over others need to be careful not to take their authority lightly. We see in Scripture that disobedience on the part of those in spiritual authority over others affects the whole group over which they have authority (e.g., Israel's kings). In the case of Achan (Josh. 7), the sin of one person, apparently not in leadership, can also affect the relationship of the whole nation to the Lord. Inherent in this understanding of spiritual authority is the fact that pastors and other leaders are always targeted for greater spiritual attack, hence the need for greater prayer protection. Consider the difference in impact if an usher in the church has a sexual affair with a member of the church versus the pastor having an affair with that same member. If Satan can bring a leader down in sin, the damage to others is obviously much more severe.

But it is not just the publicly exposed sin that is a serious threat here. More damage is being done in the Body of Christ with secret sins among Christian leaders than could even begin to be measured. Just because something is secret doesn't mean it does no damage. In fact, that is often the rationale behind our sin. Since no one knows, we think, no one is being hurt. But Satan can and does use secret sins to keep a spiritual leader powerless and ineffective, just as easily as he can use exposure of that sin to bring destruction. Our hunch is that Satan often works hard to keep a Christian leader with secret sin in place. The reason is that secret sin robs leaders of their spiritual power and authority. Therefore, Satan would not want to expose them and run the risk of their being replaced with a person who is spiritually clean and whose spiritual authority is uncompromised. Obviously, it serves Satan's purposes to expose secret sin sometimes. But exposure could also be God's way of dealing with "sin in the camp."

Another example of the use of authority is the role of the parent over a child. When parents dedicate children to God or Satan, they give authority to their master to work in and through those children's lives. In the case of a child dedicated to Satan, this authority, unless identified and renounced, may continue as a demonic presence for the child's lifetime. We often find ourselves dealing with demons given access to a person as a child dedicated in a pagan temple to family gods or ancestral spirits. Interestingly, sometimes these dedications were made without the child even being present. This is what happens when the grandparents of a child of Christian parents do a temple dedication of the child without the knowledge of the parents. The grandparents' spiritual authority over their grandchild becomes the access point of a demon.

Observation 4.8
Humans can be inhabited either by God's Spirit, demons or both.

Many children begin life with family and/or other demons living within them. These demons have rights in our ancestors and are passed down through our parent's bloodlines at conception. We do not know why God allows this to happen to innocent children, unless it is connected to the sin nature with which we are born. Added to this may be demons invited into us by people in authority over us (e.g. child dedications to pagan gods, persons in authority over a child inviting in demons as in cult families, or through curses spoken against us by others). Then, there is the issue of the conscious or unconscious invitation to demons to inhabit us through our habitual participation in sin, victimization, or participation in occult type activities.

The issue of whether Christians can be inhabited by demons sparks a lively debate. Most contenders against this being a possibility have had little or no experience dealing with demonized people. Working from theory rather than experience, they like to refer to Scriptures like I John 4:4: "Greater is he who is in you than he who is in the world." But this text does not speak directly to the question of the demonization of Christians and to say it does is to misinterpret and marginalize the text. The early church certainly believed that Christians could have demons, at least immediately after conversion. Eusebius, the early church historian, reports that one Christian church in the third century had, among other leaders, fifty-two exorcists.[1] The early church assumed that there were demons to deal with in nearly all new Christians.

A study of Scripture offers no conclusive support for either position concerning the demonization of Christians. In the absence of such support, therefore, we must look to those with experience in dealing with this situation in the Body of Christ. Our experience with well over a thousand deliverance sessions, plus that of every other practitioner we have spoken to or read (e.g. C. Fred Dickason, *Demon Possession and the Church*, Moody Press), proves to us that Christians can indeed be demonized even though the Holy Spirit indwells them. Those who would doubt this need only to follow us around for a few days of doing ministry and see the changed faces and lives of believers freed from demonic oppression.

We have asked ourselves how this can happen. How is it that Christians can have both the Holy Spirit and demons at the same time? We see the answer as follows. Prior to conversion, demons can occupy the spirit (the place in us where the Holy Spirit comes to dwell, also called the "heart"), the soul (mind, will, emotions), and the physical body of a person. When people invite Jesus Christ into their lives to become Lord and Savior, any demons are forced out of the human spirit by the presence of the Holy Spirit. But they can retain their previous position in the soul (mind, will, emotions) and the body. The Holy Spirit lives in the spirit of the person, while demons may reside in and influence the person from their position in the soul and body until deliverance comes in the power and authority of Jesus.

Let us add another word of clarification here to this whole debate. Most modern Bible translators have translated the Greek words related to demonic presence or control as "demon possessed." Since the Greek terms used do not imply possession, however, it is inaccurate for translators to use that phrase. The Greek terms simply refer to persons "having" demons living inside of them, so we prefer the term "demonized" to the inaccurate and misleading term "demon possession." When people use the terminology "demon possession," they are suggesting that the demons have much more control and influence than they actually do in the lives of most people. The only time "demon possession" might be appropriate would be when a shaman or Satanist deliberately calls a spirit to come and take him or her over for a period of time.

So, if asked, we would say many Christians to whom we minister are "demonized" at some level, meaning they have some demonic spirits in them from the sources suggested above, and that they are in need of deliverance from these spirits. This is far removed from saying they are "demon possessed" (See Kraft, *Defeating Dark Angels*, for further discussion).

Observation 4.9
Both God and Satan are able to provide protection for their followers.

Both God and Satan desire to protect those who are loyal to them, though the amounts of protection provided by God and Satan are not equal, nor are their motives the same. Satan wishes to protect his followers to keep them from defecting to the other side. Satan's goal in providing protection is to bind people to him, producing strongholds, arguments and obstacles "raised against the knowledge of God" (II Cor. 10:4-5). He doesn't want his followers to know the truth about God so he must hide it from them with his own deceptions. Unlike God, who protects for the good of His creatures, Satan's motives are selfish. He only protects as long as it serves his purposes to protect; then he destroys or allows to be destroyed, even those who have been faithful to him. Satan has no loyalties if they don't serve his purposes.

God provides a certain amount of protection automatically to His Creation and humankind. If He didn't, Satan would destroy all of life in his war against God. We believe there is evidence that God grants additional protection to His followers when we ask for it, though through experience we know that all who ask God for protection from evil don't necessarily get the protection they ask for every time.

God, in unique circumstances, withdrew His protection, at least partially, for a season. Job (Job 1) and Paul (II Cor. 12:7-9) had a portion of protection withdrawn from them by God for a season. Gideon, on the other hand, was granted the protection of God over the whole nation of Israel until his death, even though he himself had become apostate (Jdgs. 8:28).

Observation 4.10
There is a relationship between the amount of human support God or Satan has and the ability of each to successfully attack the opposing kingdom.

Frank Peretti captures this observation powerfully in the selections from *This Present Darkness* that were quoted at the beginning of Chapter One. There, the angels of light and the angels of darkness are poised, ready for the final battle for the city of Ashton. But the angels of light are not released to begin the battle, because there is not enough "prayer cover" by "the faithful." Only when enough intercessors are awakened by the Spirit and are on their knees releasing prayer cover can the battle begin, and ultimately be won. Though his books are fictionalized, Peretti's writing dramatically portrays many of the principles we have observed. As such, they are excellent resources to read to gain a spiritual warfare perspective, though they remain works of fiction.

Prayer is the critical dynamic here. In prayer we are seeking an intimacy with God. Then out of that intimacy we are asking God to move and then trusting in faith that He will move in response to our prayer. Prayer is the "human support" that God responds to and is empowered by. In prayer, hopefully, we are lining up our wills with God's will. Prayer should then naturally flow into obedience, and as mentioned earlier (see Observation 4.4), obedience releases God's blessings for us. When there are large numbers of people praying and obeying God, spiritual power is released and the Lord is then in a position to order an attack with the promise of winning.

Under Joshua's leadership, the people of Israel in general, and their leaders in particular, usually listened for and followed God's orders. They attacked only when God said to do so and therefore won the battles. Earlier in Israel's history, Moses gained great authority with God through his obedience. In spite of the fact that the people were not necessarily with him at first, and he was a reluctant leader, Moses' obedience made him usable by God. The prophets of Baal were defeated when God used Elijah in the authoritative position of the Prophet of Israel (I Kings 18) who listened and did what God told him to do.

With Moses and with Gideon, prior obedience set the stage for them to be used by God. Continuing obedience guaranteed success for their battles. On the other hand, note what happened in the case of Joshua's army attempting to take the city of Ai (Joshua 7). Through the disobedience of Achan, the power of God was compromised and the battle to initially take Ai lost. When Joshua was on his face seeking understanding, God told him that Israel had been made "liable to destruction. I will not be with you anymore unless you destroy whatever among you is devoted to destruction. ...You cannot stand against your enemies until you deal with it" (Joshua 7:12-13). Joshua knew that something had caused the loss because of God's favor on him. He immediately sought out "the sin in the camp" and dealt with it severely. Then Joshua had total victory over the city of Ai and destroyed it as God had commanded in the first place.

As mentioned earlier, "sin in the camp" is often a much more subtle way of Satan gaining victory and control than a full frontal attack which everyone can see and respond to. One can only ponder again how often Satan is empowered by secret sins in the lives of pastors and leaders to render their churches powerless and defenseless. Secret sin is more akin to termites attacking the support walls of a house. No one knows they are there until the damage is done, and then it is too late. Such is the insidious nature of secret sin.

Observation 4.11
Those related to God or Satan can use a variety of methods to transmit spiritual power.

Spiritual power can be transmitted in a variety of ways. Some of the vehicles most frequently used are words (such as prayer, blessing, cursing, dedications), touch (laying on of hands as in II Tim 1:6), being in sacred places (such as temples, churches, shrines), and possession of empowered objects (such as objects dedicated to a spiritual power like crosses, crucifixes, religious artifacts, idol statues, black magic paraphernalia or cursed objects like voodoo dolls). Spiritual power can be imparted to an object through words or rituals. The possession of such things then imparts the spiritual power of the object to the possessor. Hence the danger of possessing pagan artifact. This is in part the fascination through history with the search for the Holy Grail, or the present day interest in the Shroud of Turin. Possessing the object could promise one a share of the supposed spiritual power it contains.

Words can be used to impart power. God usually uses words to transmit His power to humans and empowers us to do the same. Since Satan is a copier, he also uses words to transmit his power. The power of a father's blessing is illustrated in the competition between Jacob and Esau to get the blessing of their father Isaac (Gen. 27). We also see the power of blessings in the blessing of Jacob over his sons before his death (Gen. 49), and Moses laying his hands on Joshua to pass on the mantle of leadership (Deut. 34:9). We have also seen the power of parental words to place curses over a child. We cannot say enough about the power of parents to bless their children. Many of those we see for prayer ministry would not be there if their parents, especially their fathers, had only known how to bless them as children, and then bless them as men and women.

In addition, dedicated people, buildings or objects can carry the power of the spirit being in whose name they were dedicated. Two thousand Buddhist monks were dedicated recently in our city. These monks were dedicating their lives to serving Buddhism and (unconsciously) the gods (demons) that govern the Buddhist religion. Spiritual power was imparted to the new priests by the blessing of the Dalai Lama, the spiritual leader of one Buddhist sect, who was visiting our city for that purpose. We could only begin to imagine the demonic power surrounding the convention center where this religious ceremony took place. Then we were shocked when we heard the news report that the mayor of our city was giving the Dalai Lama the symbolic keys to our city.

Another warning that needs to be noted here concerns using spiritual power that you don't have the authority to use. The experience of the sons of Sceva in Acts 19:13-16 warns us that those who attempt to transmit the power of God without the authority to do so place themselves in danger. People who are not in a saving relationship with Jesus can place themselves in harm's way without realizing it as the sons of Sceva did, if they try to use an authority that is not theirs.

Those who dabble in the occult, even if naively, need to recognize that they are exposing themselves to a variety of ways Satan transmits his spiritual power into their lives. They may not realize the danger they are putting themselves in and will end up paying a high price for their ignorance.

Observation 4.12
People have the right to switch from one allegiance to the other.

People who have pledged their allegiance to God or Satan have the choice to take that allegiance back from one spiritual power and give it to the other. Those who have been dedicated to God as children through infant baptism or dedication by those in authority over them can, by neglecting that commitment and living as members of Satan's kingdom (even if unconsciously), change their allegiance. God's rules obviously allow this as evidenced by the reality that in many Christian families children abandon the faith of their parents.

The reverse is just as true as children dedicated to Satan can leave the pagan religion they were dedicated to and choose to follow the true God. One difference here is that those who were dedicated to Satan through pagan religions and then choose Christ usually need help from others to get rid of the demons that were invited into them at their dedication to the false gods.

Even after coming to Christ and reuniting our human spirits with God's Spirit, Satan can still interfere in the Christian's life under certain circumstances. When we sin, we give him permission to harm our fellowship with God until we repent of that sin. If we wallow in sin, we open ourselves up to demonization and usually need help to get free again. If Christians could just realize the seriousness of a casual approach to sin perhaps we would be less quick to seize the opportunities Satan offers us for our pleasure and his victory.

Notes

1. Eusebius, *Ecclesiastical History*, VI, 43. II., as quoted by Stephen Neill, *A History of Christian Missions* (New York, NY: Penguin Books, 1990), p. 31.

———◆———

CHAPTER SEVEN

PRINCIPLE FIVE:
Cultural Forms
Can Be Empowered

In addition to the empowerment of humans, we also must confront the issue of the empowerment of cultural forms such as words, material objects, places, and buildings. Blessings and curses, talismans and shrines, rituals and music, all fit under this principle. However, the empowerment of words (see Observation 4.10) is basic to this whole principle. Words usually serve as the vehicles through which other items are empowered.

Observation 5.1
Physical objects can be dedicated to spirit beings.

In many societies it is customary for those who make implements used for worship, work, decoration, or other functions to dedicate them to their gods or spirits. Many groups of Christians dedicate articles used in worship routinely, including sanctuary furnishings, crosses, crucifixes, anointing oil, the communion elements, and holy water. Once dedicated, such objects may carry the power of God, as did the Ark of the Covenant and other sacred objects in Old Testament times, and Paul's handkerchiefs and aprons in the New Testament (Acts 19:12).

The Ark of the Covenant was the physical symbol of God's presence with Israel. So powerful was it that when the priest carried it into the flood swollen Jordan River the waters stopped and the children of Israel crossed over on dry land into Canaan (Josh. 3). No one was allowed to touch it or look into it. To do so was to touch the presence of God and death was the result (I Sam. 6:19).

When the Philistines, who were defeating the Israelites in battle, heard that the Ark had been brought up from Shiloh into the camp of the Israelites, "the Philistines were afraid. A god has come into the camp," they said. "We are in trouble" (I Sam. 4:7). But the Philistines recovered from their fear, defeated the army of Israel and captured the Ark of the Covenant. Israel's response was, "the glory has departed from Israel, because the ark of God has been captured" (I Sam. 4:22). But the Philistines did not know that empowered items in the hands of the other side could cause negative consequences.

The Philistines took the Ark to Ashdod and put it next to the statue of the city god Dagon as a symbol of their victory. The next morning the statue of Dagon was knocked over on its face before the Ark. They set it back up but, the next morning it was not only knocked over again, its head and arms were broken off as well. Then devastation and plagues hit the Philistines in Ashdod and every other city to which they kept moving the Ark, until they finally, in fear, returned it to the Israelites.

Similar to the prededing story about the international relief agency which had it offices decorated with pagan worship
items, numerous have been the stories of Christian travelers
and missionaries who have found demonic disruption in their
homes until they got rid of pagan artifacts purchased abroad.
Our colleague, C. Peter Wagner, had such an experience in
his home until he got rid of a group of religious items he and
his wife had brought back with them from Bolivia. Unknown
to them, these items had been dedicated to evil spirits and
they innocently brought demonic power centers right into their
living room.[1]

In the New Testament, objects such as Paul's handkerchiefs and aprons conveyed God's power for healing and
deliverance. Following the model of James 5:14, we routinely
find anointing oil that has been blessed in the name of the
Lord Jesus Christ to be effective in healing and lessening the
power of demons. Some people have found it helpful to bless
such things as water, salt, a cross, a Bible, or the communion
elements and use them for similar purposes.

We once had trouble in freeing a woman from a difficult
and recurring cough, the source of which could not be deter-
mined medically. What was finally revealed through a word
of knowledge was that the cough was tied to an event of repeated sexual abuse as a child. The inner child part of her was
trying to cough up the dirtiness she felt inside. Again, through
a word of knowledge, we mixed a glass of water with a pinch
of salt (water and salt represent the two ingredients our bodies
must have or we will die within a few days). We blessed it
and dedicated it to Jesus. By this process it became "holy
water." When the water was drunk, we declared in the name
of Jesus that it was breaking the power of the enemy over her
because of the abuse. We also declared in the name of Jesus
that the holy water was breaking the power of the cough by

washing out of her any traces of dirtiness and evil that had been put into her body. The cough, while not completely healed, was reduced to almost nothing immediately. After a few more ministry sessions to deal with the areas of pain tied to the abuse, the cough disappeared completely.

Lest we fall into the error of beginning to think magically about such things, let us remember that the power is not initially in the object itself. The power can come from God or Satan and is merely *conveyed* through the dedicated and blessed item. A Satanist could have satanic power to "bless" the salt and water for evil purposes. In this ministry session this "holy water" worked because the word of knowledge from the Lord suggested that *this* was the way to deal with *this* problem in *this* person. Our obedience to this revelation from God resulted in her freedom.

One of our colleagues once told a father whose son was having a problem with swearing that he should have the son swallow salt that had been blessed in the name of Jesus and that would break the power of the demon behind the swearing. He suggested this because it had worked once before in another similar situation with great success. The father had the son do this, and the lack of results not only weakened the faith of the son in the power of God to help him, it seriously threatened the credibility of our ministry in the eyes of the father. We refer to this as "the Moses Mistake" in our ministry training sessions. Just because something worked one time under the direction of the Holy Spirit, does not mean you can arbitrarily repeat it in a similar situation and expect the same results.

Observation 5.2
Words used with the authority of God or Satan,

especially blessings or curses, are empowered to release reward or punishment in the human realm.

Words are, in and of themselves, neutral. The words we use, however, whether in thought or verbal form, can get empowered by either God or Satan, based on our intent or invitation. Words that form blessings and curses are ordinarily empowered by the one to whom the speaker is committed (see Observation 4.11).

To bless someone in the name of Jesus is to invoke the presence of the full nature and authority of Jesus for the person being blessed. To curse someone is to invoke the presence of the full nature and evil power of Satan against the person being cursed. The words we use, whether to bless or to curse, are the "property" of those who utter them. In Luke 9 and 10, Jesus sent His disciples out to witness, commanding them to bless a home first, then to retract the blessing if they were not welcomed there. The fact that the disciples had given the blessing meant that they could also retract it. The power God invested their words with was under their control. Christians can specifically bless persons with things like peace and joy, or the "desires of their heart." We can also bless objects such as cars, homes, offices, and other things with protection from the enemy's interference.

A problem area that often comes up in ministry is the power of self-cursing. We all are profoundly gifted at saying negative and mean things to ourselves and about ourselves. The things we say against ourselves can be empowered by the enemy because they are supporting his strategy to destroy us. We all have things about our bodies or other parts of us that we do not like and wish were different. But when we curse these things, we unintentionally release Satan to attack those parts of ourselves. The reverse is also true. When we use our words to bless ourselves we release God's power over our lives and do His will by blessing what he has given us. We often suggest to clients, who have cursed their bodies, that every day when they take a bath, as they are toweling off, they bless each part of their body as they dry it. Such an exercise certainly puts our focus right. We can break our demonically empowered self-curses by simply renouncing them in the name of Jesus and then refusing to allow ourselves to speak or believe them again.

Another place where the demonic empowerment of words is seen is in the power of curses spoken against us. We routinely minister to people who believe that someone practicing witchcraft has placed a curse against them and they want our help to break it. We usually tell them to verbally renounce the curse in the power and authority of Jesus' name and then send it back from where it came as a blessing and not a curse. With words curses are made, and with words curses are broken! Most people are amazed that breaking the power of a curse over us is that simple, because they forget who has the most power.

Most Christians have no idea of the curses being spoken against their pastors and leaders by satanic cults in their communities. Cults have "prayer lists" and "prayer rallies" just like Christians, but for opposing purposes. Of great consequence to the Body of Christ is the fact that many Christians routinely speak curses against their pastors and leaders with the criticisms and gossip they engage in. Words get empowered—for good or evil! We had best watch what we say lest we inadvertently serve Satan and his purposes.

Another example of the empowerment of words is the

existence of "inner vows." Identified by John and Paula Sandford in their book *The Transformation of the Inner Man*, inner vows are directives we speak into our inner being, usually as children, that become demonically empowered, rigid obstructions in our nature. Their specific purpose is to hold us to feel, think and act only in accordance with a rule set by the inner vow.[2] Examples of inner vows could be beliefs like: "I will never let someone hurt me like that again," or "Never trust men, they will always leave you," or "Never trust a woman," or "Never let anyone see you cry," or "Don't ever trust God," or "Don't feel or show emotion."

Once stated, inner vows usually become demonically empowered, holding us captive to this inner direction based on old hurts and wounds in our hearts. We put the inner vow there in innocence to protect our hearts from pain. Satan then holds the inner vow in place to keep us from life. Like self-curses, once identified, inner vows can be renounced in the name of Jesus, repented for, and spiritually removed from our hearts and minds. The person will then have to work at overcoming the old behavior patterns that were established by the inner vows to gain total freedom. But this change of habitual thinking and behaving is usually more easily accomplished without the inner vow in place.

Words are also used for many other spiritual purposes. Words used to dedicate someone or something carry the power of the one in whose name they are dedicated. Words used in preaching sermons or witnessing to someone become empowered by God when they are dedicated to Him. But remember, Satan counterfeits every method God uses. Those nicely dressed, neatly trimmed young men in airports who are offering free books to read "about faith" are very often not Christians as one might expect, by rather are cult members witnessing for Satan. And he empowers their witnessing just as the Holy Spirit empowers ours!

Observation 5.3
Other nonmaterial cultural forms can also be empowered by God or Satan.

Music is an obvious cultural form that impacts all our lives. We often see music empowered through its dedication to either God or Satan. Rituals, traditional ceremonies, dances, and other worship activities are often empowered as well. The blessing we feel in Christian worship is likely due to the fact that God does "inhabit our praise." In worship to God, the desire is to be drawn to God our Father and feel His pleasure and presence in our worship.

Christian music is effective in conveying God's love and power to those who listen to it. It lifts us up and focuses our mind on God. This can especially be helpful when one is late and caught in rush hour traffic. Christian music played in our homes and cars is also effective in suppressing enemy activity and protecting against satanic attacks in those places. Nothing can be better for children and young people than listening to Christian music, even if it is Christian rock music. If your kids like music, just be sure you know what they are listening to. Not all secular music is empowered by Satan. But the lyrics may not carry the kind of messages you want influencing your kids.

At the same time there are music and music groups that are openly dedicating their music to Satan and his purposes. Theirs is a kind of satanic worship music that has young people by the thousands worshiping at their pagan altars of ego and debauchery. It is interesting to note that most of the gunmen in the series of recent high school shooting incidents all have one common element—they all listened to the music of a current rock musician whose lyrics celebrate death, blood, the killing of policemen, and Satan, among other things. Such music conveys satanic power and entrapment to its devotees. They often listen to it under the influence of drugs or alcohol, which leaves their minds open to whatever Satan wants to dump into their souls. And we have already discussed the occultic and demonic themes of many of the popular video games that young children are drawn to play today.

Also consider the whole national shame of abortion, or the homosexual movement in America. Or consider the casual attitude toward all forms of sexual behavior outside of marriage. We hope you were as surprised as we were that the majority of Americans were not that upset about the President of the United States having a sexual relationship with a woman young enough to be his daughter. Equally distressing was his ability to "define" away his sin instead of genuinely repenting for it.

All of these things represent the empowerment of nonmaterial cultural forms. It is Satan controlling the mindsets of a society to erode the values and truths that God built into his creation. We had best be paying attention to what Satan is doing.

Observation 5.4
Buildings can be invested with spiritual power by God or Satan.

Both Christians and non-Christians intentionally dedicate buildings to their divinities. Church buildings, homes, shrines, and other places can be purposefully "inhabited" by whatever "spirit" is invited to dwell there. Buildings can be consciously dedicated to God or Satan. We also believe that buildings can be "unofficially" dedicated through the intent of their owners. Buildings can become satanically empowered through regular use for evil purposes such as prostitution, gambling, pornography, homosexual activity, financial swindling, abortion clinics, or occult meetings.

It has been our experience that it can be dangerous for Christians to enter certain buildings without claiming God's protection. These would include Mormon churches, Masonic lodges, pagan shrines and temples, occult and New Age bookstores, fortune-telling centers, some establishments dealing with health foods, environmental concerns and non-Christian martial arts, offices of occult groups and sin-enhancing organizations, and other buildings used for satanic purposes. We are not suggesting a paranoid fear grip us, but rather we suggest caution and wisdom when around these kind of places. If you do have to enter them, you should always claim God's protection.

As Christians, we must also not forget our authority over the places were we live and serve. We were once consulted by a mission leader concerning one of his colleagues who routinely became disruptive during mission meetings. We asked this leader if he had spiritually cleansed the room prior to each meeting. He had not, but at our suggestion started to. He later reported the disruptive person's behavior changed dramatically when he was in that meeting place after that. Something spiritual in the room had been removed.

We have had similar conversations with teachers concerning disruptive children in their classrooms. Once the teachers began asserting their spiritual authority over the classrooms before the kids arrived, and began praying spiritual blessings over the children who were disruptive, the mood in the classroom changed dramatically.

Observation 5.5
Animals can be empowered with spiritual power.

While we do not think of animals as having souls, there is some kind of connection between the animal kingdom and the spirit kingdom. In Mark 5, Jesus sent a legion of demons into a herd of nearby pigs. The narrative reports that the evil spirits in the man begged Jesus to let them go into the pigs. When He allowed it, they left the man and entered the pigs. The narrative then reports an amazing thing—the pigs that had been feeding peacefully, suddenly reacted to being entered by the demons and rushed off a nearby cliff and were killed. No explanation is given as to why this happened. Maybe the spirits were unable to kill the demonized man because his will was strong enough to resist them. Therefore, they killed the pigs, which they could control, to show their power. Or perhaps the pigs sensed the presence of the evil enter them and ran over the cliff in their reaction to the demons coming into them. Whatever the explanation, the pigs had a reaction to the evil power that entered them.

Scripture records other examples of animals being used by God. Numbers 22:22-35 tells the story of the prophet Balaam and his donkey. Balaam was going to see the King of Moab who wished him to put a curse on the people of Israel who had moved into the land. The account says that on the way to see the King of Moab, three times the donkey upon which Balaam was riding saw an angel standing in the road blocking the way. Twice the donkey went around the angel, only to be beaten by Balaam for going off the road, one time crushing Balaam's foot against a stone wall trying to go around the angel. The third time the donkey saw the angel blocking the way there was no room to go around and the donkey lay down in the road. When Balaam started to beat the donkey, the Lord gave the donkey the power to speak to Balaam and question the legitimacy of the beatings. After their conversation, the Lord allowed Balaam to see the angel that had been blocking his way and discovered the donkey had actually saved his life.

One could wonder too about the quail that the Lord sent each evening to feed the children of Israel for forty years in the desert. Or the fact that at the baptism of Jesus the Holy Spirit descended on him "like a dove" (Matt. 3:16). One can wonder, too, how it was that Noah could gather pairs of all the animals, some of them natural enemies, and keep them peacefully on the Ark for what was probably more than a year.

We also believe that animals have a sensitivity to the spirit world. Black cats are identified with the occult and desired by cult groups for their activities. Obviously, there is some spiritual motivation on the part of the cult. We think that sometimes animals sense or see things that we can't as humans. We have a hunch that the negative reactions that some animals have to some people has to do with what they sense concerning the spiritual activity around that person.

Once in a ministry session with a man, one of our team members was accompanied by her large dog. The dog was resting quietly beside her while we conducted the ministry session. During the deliverance part of the ministry we challenged a spirit of witchcraft to come to attention. At the command to the demon the dog suddenly sat up, hair bristled on the back of his neck, he looked at the man and started growling. The dog stayed that way until we cast the demon out, at which time the dog laid back down and went back to sleep.

The dog was obviously sensing or seeing what we were dealing with in the spirit realm.

While our churches do not participate, some churches have an annual blessing service for animals where pet owners bring their pets to the church for the priest to bless them. We are not sure what the impact of such a service is on the animals, but we know the owners are blessed by it.

Notes

1. C. Peter Wagner, *Warfare Prayer* (Ventura, CA: Regal Books, 1992), pp. 81-82.
2. John and Paula Sandford, *The Transformation of the Inner Man* (Plainfield, NJ: Bridge, 1982), pp. 191-205.

CHAPTER EIGHT

PRINCIPLE SIX:
Territories and Organizations
Can Be Subject to Spirit Power

There is a chain of command and variety of function in the spirit world as God and Satan apparently impart levels of power and authority to their hierarchy of angels. Ephesians 6:12 describes at least a portion of the demonic hierarchy. The *Good News Bible* labels them as rulers, authorities, and cosmic powers. In the same passage the *New International Version* labels them rulers, authorities, powers of the dark world, and spiritual forces of evil in the heavenly realms.

Whatever the terminology, it is clear that a hierarchy exists in the demonic kingdom. In Daniel 10, reference is made to high-level satanic princes who ruled over Persia and Greece. They are titled the Prince of Persia and the Prince of Greece. We can note that Lucifer initially held a very high rank in God's army of angels until his rebellion, suggested in parallel applications of Isaiah 14:12-15 and Ezekiel 28:11-19. While these passages are literally directed at the kings of Babylon and Tyre, they also appear to describe how Satan lost his position in God's army and became the adversary of human-kind.

In Scripture we also have references to high-level angels serving God. While the hierarchy that exists among God's angels is not specifically delineated in Scripture, we can rightly assume that such a structure does exist. This is based on the assumption that because Satan usually copies and counterfeits what God does, in creating his hierarchy of demons he was probably replicating what he had experienced in God's army.

Only two of God's angels are named, Michael and Gabriel. Michael is titled an archangel (Jude 9). While Gabriel is never titled, his function is that of being a messenger of God to hu-mankind (Dan. 8:16, 9:21, Luke 1:19,26). Gabriel describes his unique position in God's hierarchy when he says of him-self, "I stand in the presence of God, who sent me to speak to you and tell you this good news" (Luke 1:19). There is also reference to cherubim (Ezek. 10) and seraphim (Is. 6:2,6) whose functions seem to be related to the Temple and to wor-ship. It is also suggested that each of the churches of Revelation 1-3 seems to have had a cosmic-level angel from God in charge of each church in some way.

Since all authority is delegated authority, God can assign different levels of power to different levels of angels in His Kingdom, and Satan can do the same in his kingdom. We assume, then, that some of God's angels and Satan's demons serve on the cosmic level and others at the ground level. The cosmic-level angels and demons seem to be more powerful than ground-level angels and demons. They also seem to deal more specifically with groupings of people (e.g., nations, cit-ies and institutions) than with individuals.

We often refer to these more powerful cosmic-level spir-its as "territorial spirits," even though it is the people, not the land, within a territory that are their primary focus. While most people utilize this territorial designation for demonic spirits, we think the term just as appropriately describes the function of God's high-level angels. There are cosmic-level, satanic "territorial" spirits assigned to promote Satan's agenda over specific territories, buildings or organizations. But at the same time we assume that God has His high-level "territorial" angels assigned to guard Christian churches and organizations and their properties, and promote God's agenda (see Observation 6.5). Which side succeeds in the territorial battle is greatly dependent on us (see Observation 4.2, 4.3, 4.10).

If we were to seek to diagram how the two opposing hierarchies would parallel each other it would look something like this:

GOD'S ARMY		SATAN'S ARMY
Archangel Michael (and possibly Gabriel)	vs.	Archangel Satan
Cherubim	vs.	Unknown Demon
Seraphim	vs.	Unknown Demon
Unnamed Angels	vs.	Rulers/Principalities
Unnamed Angels	vs.	Authorities/Powers
Unnamed Angels	vs.	Cosmic Powers/Mighty Powers of Darkness
Unnamed Angels (working from outside humans with the Holy Spirit who works from outside unbelievers, but also from inside believers)	vs.	Ground-Level Demons (working from inside humans)

A point often overlooked, but illustrated in this diagram, is the fact that the battle is not between God and Satan, for Satan is not God's equal. God, through Jesus' death on the Cross and His Resurrection has already defeated Satan. The battle is, therefore, waged for the hearts of humankind between Satan and his army and God's angelic army led by the Holy Spirit. And we as humans must make a choice as to who has our allegiance. For whoever has our allegiance, has our hearts.

Cosmic-Level Satanic Spirits

There seem to be at least five types of cosmic-level satanic spirits at work in the heavenlies over us. Below them are at least three types of "ground-level" satanic spirits at work, probably governed by cosmic-level spirits in the satanic chain-of-command. The following list is not necessarily in order of the level of power wielded by the various types or not.

1. **Territorial spirits.** These spirits are in charge of territories such as nations (Dan. 10:13, 20), regions, cities, and the like.

2. **Institutional and Religion spirits.** These spirits are in charge of the non-Christian religions (e.g. Buddhism, Hinduism, Islam, Mormonism, Christian Science, Scientology, etc.), occult organizations (e.g. Freemasonry, New Age) and are assigned to Christian churches and parachurch ministries as well.

3. **Vice spirits.** These spirits are assigned to promote and empower vices such as prostitution, pornography, gambling, homosexuality, abortions, and the like.

4. **Nature, Household, and Cultural Objects spirits.** These are the spirits that inhabit homes and sections of homes (e.g. kitchen gods, bedroom gods), rocks, trees, bodies of water, dedicated items such as work implements (e.g. axes, tools), canoes, and other cultural objects including religious objects, and nonmaterial items like music and rituals.

5. **Ancestral spirits.** These are the spirits that deceive people into believing that their dead ancestors are still functioning in the society in which they once lived.

Ground-Level Satanic Spirits

There are at least three types of ground-level satanic spirits that can inhabit people.

1. **Family spirits.** These are inherited by children from parents and go by the names of the father's and mother's families.

2. **Occult spirits.** These live in the members of occult organizations and non-Christian religions such as Freemasonry, New Age, Scientology, Mormonism, Islam, Hinduism, etc.

3. **Ordinary spirits.** These are the "footsoldiers" whose job it is to reinforce negative emotions such as fear, hatred, shame, depression, unforgiveness, anger, lust, and the like. These also include spirits such as death, rebellion, violence, abuse, pride, suicide, abortion, and so forth (see Charles Kraft's book, *Defeating Dark Angels*, [Servant Publications], for a longer list of demon names).

Observation 6.1

God or Satan's cosmic-level spirits seem to exert a "force field" influence over territories, buildings, and organizations.

It is interesting to note that sinful human activities and businesses such as prostitution, gambling, abortion, pornography, homosexuality, and occult bookstores are often clustered in certain sections of cities. This suggests that there might be ruling spirits in charge of those areas, assisting in their success. As a response to this awareness, there is a new movement among Christians aimed at identifying the enemy's activity in an identified city by "spiritually mapping" geographical areas to detect discernible patterns of demonic activities in these areas. These patterns reveal the probable spirits in charge of those areas and suggest a strategy of focused prayer against them.

This focused prayer by Christians against the agenda of the satanic territorial spirits then releases God's territorial spirits to attack Satan's agenda for a city (see Observation 4.10). We know of one church that began having members sit across the street from an adult bookstore in their neighborhood to pray against its presence in their area daily. Their prayer was focused at "binding" the spiritual power of evil over the bookstore. Within a few months the store closed for no known human reason (for further information on spiritual mapping, see C. Peter Wagner's *Breaking Strongholds in Your City* [Regal Books] and John Dawson's *Taking Our Cities for God* [Creation House]).

Such "force field" influence also extends to individuals within a territory. As pointed out in II Corinthians 4:4, our enemy is able to keep the minds of unbelievers in the dark, blinding them to the truth. Indeed, the verse goes on to indicate that Satan is even able to counter the force field of God. "[Satan] keeps them from seeing the light shining on them, the light that comes from the Good News about the glory of Christ, who is the exact likeness of God" (I Cor. 4:5). So we assume that at least part of the assignment of cosmic-level spirits is to keep the truth of God from the areas they guard. But we also know that God's cosmic-level angels can be empowered to defeat the enemy's strategy.

It is this "blinding activity" of cosmic level spirits that Ed Silvoso and others are now learning to nullify through cosmic-level spiritual warfare prayer. This is where groups of Christians gather to specifically pray for the release of God's power against the power of the cosmic-level evil spirits assigned to the city being evangelized.

Especially in Latin America (e.g. Argentina, Guatemala, Colombia) we are seeing impressive numbers of conversions and church growth statistics following intense spiritual warfare prayer campaigns by Christians against the identified territorial spirits of a city. Often the religious leaders and evangelists will not even begin a series of evangelistic crusades in a city until they are satisfied that the spiritual power of God over a city exceeds the spiritual power of the enemy. Reminiscent of Peretti's description of spiritual warfare among angels in the opening of this book, once the enemy spirits are "defeated and bound" with a greater spiritual power, the evangelistic campaigns begin in earnest with incredible results.[1]

Observation 6.2
Spirit beings must have legal rights to exert authority over territories, organizations and individuals.

Spirit beings must have legal rights to the territories they have authority over. Such rights are given to them through the allegiances, dedications, and behavior of the humans who now use and have used the territories and organizations in the past.

Territories and organizations can be consciously or even unconsciously dedicated to the kingdom of God or the kingdom of Satan. Like buildings, they can also be dedicated by the purposes for which they are used, whether to glorify God or to glorify Satan. When a place or organization has been dedicated, that dedication can be weakened, sometimes even broken, by subsequent opposite usage. One need not wonder whose spirits stand guard over a church that calls itself Christian, but endorses abortion and homosexuality.

When one considers the spiritual impact of slavery on the southern United States this observation comes alive. The majority of the people who lived in the South in the mid-1800s, including the slaves themselves, seldom questioned the legitimacy or spiritual rightness of this practice. It was just accepted as "the way things are." Even the churches, the "spiritual gatekeepers" of the community, supported slavery as an acceptable practice, some even calling it God-ordained.

This attitude and action empowered the high level demonic spirits behind slavery to strengthen its hold over the minds of the people. Even though the Civil War ended slavery as an institution, the demon-empowered mindset that held it in place for two hundred years is still expressed today in the experience of racism. The racist mindset in America is still strong, especially in the "Deep South," where slavery had its greatest grip on the society. While slavery as an institution has been abolished, racism is still a spiritual disease that infects a large segment of the population of the United States.

While the demonic power behind racism has been weakened by reconciliation services (see Observation 6.3), in which repentance and forgiveness between races and societies is expressed by leaders from all sides, it still has a grip on the American mindset and spirit. We think the power for this is high-level demonic spirits assigned to the slavery mindset.

In an American community we conducted a seminar in a church in which strange things were happening. We learned that the church and a nearby high school had been built on an ancient Indian burial ground. Usage of the land for Christian purposes did not in and of itself seem to break the power over the land. Until the power given to the enemy over those territories long ago by evil activities is broken by the power of God, usually through repentance, Satan will continue to have great ability to interfere with God's activities in those places.

Demonic spirits also can claim legal rights to inhabit humans. In our deep level healing prayer sessions we often are called on to deliver people from the presence of demons in their lives.

Demons enter a person typically in one of four ways. They come in generationally through a person's bloodlines (see Observation 2.5). They can enter by invitation of the person, as in the case of occultic or satanic cult involvement (see Observation 2.6). They can enter through the invitation of a person in authority over another, as in the case of a child dedicated to a pagan god, family spirit, or to Satan as in the cases of cult-loyal families (see Observation 4.11). And they can enter through our choices to hold on to the "garbage" in our lives, created through emotional and spiritual woundedness, unforgiveness, anger, fear, anxiety, shame, and various other negative emotions (see Observation 4.8).

Our formula is "Where you have garbage, you have rats (demons). If you get rid of the rats (deliverance) and don't get rid of the garbage, the rats will return. If you want to get rid of the rats, get rid of the garbage first, and then get rid of the rats. Then the rats won't come back." That is why we believe that inner healing prayer to deal with the emotional and spiritual "garbage" of our lives must usually precede deliverance.

When we are doing a deliverance ministry with a person and encounter a demon, we only request information from demons to assist us in inner healing. From the demon we essentially only want to know the answer to three questions: 1) "How did you get into this person?" 2) "What do you do in this person/What is your job/What do you say to this person?" and 3) "What legal right do you have to be here now?"

It is the answer to this last question that is critical because the rules seem to be that if a demon has a legal right to be in a person it doesn't have to leave until that legal right is cancelled. Under pressure from the Holy Spirit, demons will usually declare their legal right to be in the person, a right that is then quickly cancelled, and the demon can then be successfully ordered out of the person. While we acknowledge that demons are liars, the information we receive under this ministry model, done in the authority of Christ, is usually very accurate. For further explanation about how demons work and the deliverance model we used to defeat them, see Charles Kraft's *Defeating Dark Angels* (Servant Publications).

Observation 6.3
The rules for breaking the power of cosmic-level satanic spirits are parallel to those for breaking the power of ground-level satanic spirits over individuals.

The dedication to Satan of a territory can be broken when people deal with "group garbage" through repentance, the unity of Christians (especially Christian leaders), righteousness, and other acts of obedience to God, followed by confronting the spirits in intercessory prayer.

With individuals infested with demons, we need to look for and clean out the "garbage" that gives satanic spirits legal rights in the person. For territories, it is crucial to find and break the power of commitments, dedications, curses, and sins that have been committed on the land, as well as agreements made consciously or unconsciously by those in authority over the land, that gave legal rights to the enemy.

Examples of such territory would be cities known to have been dedicated by Freemasons (e.g. Washington D.C. and several Argentine cities), places where blood has been shed unjustly (e.g. Wounded Knee, South Dakota), and sections of cities given over to violence, pornography, prostitution, abortion clinics, and homosexuality. Just as with individuals, being cleansed from sin is an important step in breaking the enemy's power, and is crucial to the attainment of lasting freedom. This is where the process of spiritual mapping of a city mentioned earlier becomes so critical—along with gaining knowledge of the full history of your city and your neighborhood.

The power of the cosmic-level, satanic spirits over areas infected by sinful usage can be weakened, and hopefully broken, through repentance on the part of those now in authority over those areas. We call this *identificational repentance.* It consists of contemporary representatives of groups who sinned against other groups, in the past and present, taking responsibility for the sins of their ancestors and repenting (preferably in public) to contemporary representatives of the groups wronged.

A prime example of this practice in recent years has been the racial reconciliation services where Caucasian pastors repent and ask for forgiveness from African-American pastors for the sins of slavery and racism. Then the African-American pastors repent and ask forgiveness from the Caucasian pastors for the hatred of African-Americans toward Caucasians. Other racial groups that have a history of exploitation may participate as well. Often these services include foot washing as a symbol of each group's desire to serve the other.

We also use identificational repentance in ministry sessions, standing in the place of perpetrators of evil in a person's life and repenting to victims on behalf of those who wounded them. We have each in ministry sessions repented to women and men for the sins of men toward them, being the male spiritual leaders or pastors who hurt them, fathers, brothers or even strangers, as in cases of rape. As men, we stand in the place of the perpetrators and repent for their sins against the person to whom we are ministering. If the perpetrator of evil was a woman, we get a woman to do the identificational repentance to the person who was sinned against.

The biblical model for this is the Old Testament leaders (Dan. 9) repenting for the sins of the people of Israel. Our experience is that through identificational repentance, demonic bondages over people are often broken, clearing the way for the release of forgiveness by the person toward the ones who hurt them. This act of forgiveness then opens the way for true emotional and spiritual healing in the victim.

Observation 6.4
Cosmic-level spirits seem to wield their authority over territories as defined by humans.

The impression gained by those who study and deal with territorial spirits is that there are national spirits, regional spirits, spirits over cities, and spirits over sections of cities. The fact that the guardian angel over Persia (Dan. 10:13,20) and the one over Greece (Dan. 10:21) are labeled by human territorial names would point in that direction. We will assume, as affirmed earlier, that God's cosmic-level angels are assigned similar responsibilities.

This fact is illustrated in the current move of God that has been transpiring in Argentina over the last fifteen years. In the early '80s God began to raise up a new breed of evangelists. Names like Carlos Annacondia, Omar Cabrera, Claudio Freidzon, Pablo Deiros, Edgardo Silvoso, Pablo Bottari, Eduardo Lorenzo, and Sergio Scataglini head up this list of men leading this mighty move of God. Large, citywide crusades are the hallmark of this new movement, usually referred to as the Argentine Revival because of its incredible results.

A notable characteristic of the Argentine revival crusades has been the focus on preparation through intercessory prayer. Large numbers of people are engaged in prayer before the crusades even begin. In fact, some of the evangelists and their teams go to a city weeks before a crusade is scheduled to begin the prayer preparation.

Unlike many of their American counterparts, most of these evangelists will not even begin a crusade until they feel that enough prayer cover has been released to break the bondage of the territorial spirits over the host city. Peter Wagner observes that, "No factor about the Argentine Revival is more significant than [the evangelists] taking seriously the demonic forces that attempt to throttle evangelism and to quench revival."[2] He further observes that in crusades, with thousands of people present, when Carlos Annacondia shouts out his signature war cry, "Listen to me, Satan!" in his challenge to the demonic spirits present, "All hell breaks loose," as demons manifest and deliverance teams come to minister freedom to the demonized.

The success of the Argentine Revival illustrates clearly

that cosmic-level spirits are at work to hold territories and the people in them in bondage. But the Argentine Revival also illustrates that this bondage can be broken and God's angels released to defeat Satan's angels through enough intercessory and authority praying and authority-centered preaching. If nothing else the simple numerical results of this Revival validate this point.

Observation 6.5
Cosmic-level spirits are assigned to human organizations, institutions, and activities.

In the kingdom of God we know of angels that are assigned to children (Matt. 18:10) and to churches (Rev. 1-3). We believe angels are also assigned to Christian activities such as missionary and other parachurch organizations. Institutions such as churches, seminaries, and Bible schools probably all have high-level angelic spirits assigned to them. So, possibly, do social institutions such as marriages, governments, educational institutions, and the like. Since Satan likes to copy whatever God does, it is reasonable to assume that Satan has his spirits assigned to everyone and everything that God has assigned His angels to.

It would, therefore, be reasonable to assume that both kingdoms have countering angels assigned to the same things. Likely, God assigns angelic messengers to protect a church and Satan assigns demonic spirits to destroy it. Or, God assigns angels to protect a pastor, and demons are assigned to destroy him. Probably there are also cosmic-level demonic spirits whose job it is to promote pornography, abortion, homosexuality, prostitution, and occult organizations. And there are cosmic-level angels to promote family life, marriage, pro-life activities, and moral values in a society.

Observation 6.6
There are rules that can be followed to launch attacks upon evil spirits or God's angels assigned to territories and organizations.

Both for servants of God attacking evil spiritual beings and for servants of Satan attacking God's kingdom, the most important weapon is prayer (especially intercession). God's people are not the only ones who use prayer to accomplish their purposes. God's servants and Satan's followers both regularly attack each other's kingdoms through prayer, worship and fasting, both as individuals and groups. Satanic cult groups routinely meet to pray against God's people, pastors, religious leaders, churches, and religious activities. Satanists even have their own religious holy days, some paralleling Christian holidays, and have created other religious holidays to serve their evil purposes.

A unique weapon of God's people in this battle, however, as mentioned above, is the weapon of repentance. If we have learned nothing else over the last few years of being involved in this ministry, we have learned that repentance breaks bondages and sets captives free. Interestingly, this is a weapon available only to the followers of Jesus. This is one weapon that it appears Satan can't copy and use against us, but we can use it freely against Satan, both individually and corporately. Forgiving others is another unique weapon we have in our arsenal that carries the same impact for God's people as repentance.

In ministry sessions, we have found repentance for personal, corporate, or generational sin to be a powerful tool in destroying the enemy's hold on a person. Repentance is also a good way to rid ourselves of the emotional garbage from our past that the enemy uses to hold us captive, even as believers. This way the enemy has nothing upon which to get a grip in our lives (John 14:30). We are greatly encouraged by the current wave of reconciliation meetings being held between leaders of different races and ethnic groups mentioned earlier. The identificational repentance mentioned above fits here as well (see Observation 6.3).

We heard recently that the current pastor of a large evangelical church in our area, a church that had launched a whole denomination at the turn of the century, publicly repented to the current leader of a major charismatic church and denomination. The reason for this was that when the modern Pentecostal movement began with the Azusa Street Revival in 1906, the founding pastor of the first church had publicly denounced it and declared it as unbiblical and heretical. Because the current pastor wore the spiritual mantel of the founder of his church and denomination, he felt it was time to repent for those actions of rejection and condemnation of the Pentecostal/charismatic movement and publicly bless it as a legitimate move of God.

One can only ponder the demonic chains that were loosed in the heavenlies over that church when the evangelical pastor repented to, and was forgiven by, the charismatic leader for the sins of his evangelical church and denomination against this move of God. As a side note, we later learned that the evangelical pastor was harshly criticized for his actions by his denominational leaders and later resigned his church, having found this correction to be unacceptable. Obviously, more repentance is due here.

We need to also give attention to breaking all historical and contemporary commitments, curses, and dedications holding the territory or organization in Satan's grip. We need to repent of any sins committed in that territory (see Observation 6.3 above). The praying is best done by persons with spiritual authority in that area, such as pastors or elected officials. Next, in authoritative praying, they may speak to "the spiritual powers in space" (Eph. 2:2), laying claim to the territory or organization in the name of Jesus.

Steve Nicholson, former pastor of Vineyard Christian Fellowship in Evanston, Illinois, did this in claiming a certain geographical territory for his church. Over a period of time, in prayer, he proclaimed to the satanic spirits that he was taking this specified territory for God. After some time a powerful spirit appeared to him refusing to give him as much territory as he was claiming. At this, he again asserted his claim and succeeded in breaking the power of that spirit (a spirit of witchcraft). He then saw his church double in size soon after.[3]

One cannot play a game without knowing the rules that govern the game. That is why this book was written. We are tired of seeing Christians trying to live Godly lives, and churches trying to do God's work, routinely defeated by Satan's warriors, especially when this defeat is out of simple ignorance of the rules that could give them victory. We want more people to experience the joy we get to see in people when they finally "get it!" Then we discover anew what Jesus meant when He said he came to "set the captives free" (Luke 4:18)!

Conclusion

This book represents the principles and observations that we have discovered so far in our journey into the challenging ministry of "setting captives free." These principles are not the product of academic research and reflective thought, but have been discovered "in the trenches," in the practice of ministry. But there is still much we don't know. In our attempt to discover principles and rules that govern the spiritual realm, we are probably about at the level where western scientists were in their attempts to figure out physical laws a thousand years ago.

So we readily admit that this list is not definitive, but an elementary beginning at describing the principles we see illustrated in Scripture and have experienced in our ministry of inner healing and deliverance. We are the first to acknowledge that these principles are not set in concrete, but rather are fluid and open to the addition of other ground rules and continued refinement.

We see as an ongoing task the effort to further identify and clarify the "rules" that we understand to be at work in spiritual warfare. The desired result will be that God's present army will be better equipped to fight tomorrow's battles, and that God's warriors in the future will be even better equipped to fight their spiritual wars. After all, Satan's warriors already know the rules.

One of our hopes is that as we have explicitly identified and illustrated the principles we have discovered, others can now react to them. By adding to them or challenging our observations, together we can revise our principles and together advance our understandings of this spiritual battle that surrounds us. While the thoughts of academics and theologians are welcomed, what we really desire are the comments of "practitioners," those who are doing the work of ministry, not just studying the theory and theology of it. So we welcome other "spiritual scientists" to join us on our journey.

We would hope that this book will go through countless revisions and reprints, each one a "new and improved" version of the previous one. By continuing to refine this initial list of principles and observations, we will continue to expand our understanding of the spiritual realm and better equip God's army for the battle that surrounds us. Our invitation to each of you is ...

Come and join us in the battle!

Notes
1. Edgardo Silvoso, "Prayer Power in Argentina" in C. Peter Wagner, *Engaging the Enemy* (Ventura, CA: Regal Books, 1991), pp. 109-115.
2. Carlos Annacondia, *Listen to Me, Satan!*, (Lake Mary, FL: Creation House, 1998), p. viii.
3. C. Peter Wagner, *Engaging the Enemy*, pp. 31-32.

Bibliography

Ankerberg, John and John Weldon. *The Secret Teachings of the Masonic Lodge*. Chicago: Moody Press, 1989.

Chang, Iris. *The Rape of Nanking*. Penguin Books: New York, 1998.

Enroth, Ronald. *The Lure of the Cults and New Religions*. Downers Grove, IL: InterVarsity Press, 1987.

Eusebius, *Ecclesiastical History*. VI, 43. II.

Dawson, John. *Taking Our Cities for God*. Lake Mary, FL: Creation House, 1990.

Dickason, C. Fred. *Demon Possession and the Christian*. Chicago: Moody Press, 1987.

Gibbs, Nancy. "Why? The Killing Fields of Rwanda" *Time*. May 16, 1994, Volume 143. No. 20.

Horrobin, Peter. *Healing Through Deliverance, Vol. I and II*. Kent, England: Soverign World, Ltd., 1994.

Kraft, Charles. *Behind Enemy Lines*. Ann Arbor, MI: Servant Publications: 1994.

_____. *Christianity With Power*. Ann Arbor, MI: Servant Publications. 1989.

_____. *Deep Wounds, Deep Healing*. Ann Arbor, MI: Servant Publications. 1993.

_____. *Defeating Dark Angels*. Ann Arbor, MI: Servant Publications. 1992.

_____. *I Give You. Authority*. Grand Rapids, MI: Chosen Books, 1997.

Murphy, Edward F. *The Handbook for Spiritual Warfare*. Nashville: Thomas Nelson. 1992.

Neill, Stephen. *A History of Christian Missions*. New York: Penguin Books, 1990.

Peck, M. Scott. *People of the Lie*. New York: Touchstone, 1983.

Peretti, Frank E. *This Present Darkness*. Crossways Books: Wheaton, IL. 1986.

Peterson, Eugene H. *The Message*. Colorado Springs, CO: NavPress Publishing Group. 1993, 1994, 1995.

Prince, Derek. *Blessing or Curse: You Can Chose*. Grand Rapids, MI: Chosen Books, 1998.

_____. *They Shall Expell Demons*. Grand Rapids, MI: Chosen Books. 1998.

Sandford, John and Paula. *The Transformation of the Inner Man*. Plainfield, NJ: Bridge. 1982.

_____. *Healing the Wounded Spirit*. Tulsa, OK: Victory House, 1985.

Silvoso, Edgardo, "Prayer Power in Argentina." *Engaging the Enemy*. C. Peter Wagner. Ventura, CA: Regal, 1991.

"Transformations." Video. George Otis Jr. Host. The Sentinal Group. 1999.

Wagner, C. Peter. *Breaking Strongholds in Your City*. Ventura, CA: Regal, 1993.

_____. *Engaging the Enemy*, Ventura, CA: Regal, 1991.

_____. *Warfare Prayer*. Ventura, CA: Regal, 1992.

White, Thomas B. *The Believer's Guide to Spiritual Warfare*. Ann Arbor, MI: Servant, 1990.

Wilder, E. James. *The Red Dragon Cast Down*. Grand Rapids, MI: Chosen Books, 1999.

Subject Index

Scripture Index